Charbel Tadros

The Destined Journey

Charbel Tadros was born in Brummana, Lebanon, in 1988. He teaches children with special needs as well as philosophy for high school students. He founded the Seekers Of Wisdom (www.seekersofwisdom.org) in 2006 followed by the Angels in Training program in 2010. The Destined Journey is his first spiritual novel. He lives in Brummana with his family.

The Destined Journey

CHARBEL TADROS

First edition 2010

Library of Congress Case: 1-432892151

ISBN 978-9953-0-1838-6

Cover Design by John Abou Elias and Vincenz Oberhuber

www.thedestinedjourney.com

CONTENTS

Acknowledgments

First and foremost, this book's existence between your hands wouldn't have been possible had not God, the universe, or whatever you may call the divine power willed it and coordinated through the great work of his best angels whom He sent my way. Before I thank the angels I can think of most, I'd like to thank those that I couldn't mention because, if I were to mention them, I'd need another book.

To begin with, I thank Vincenz Oberhuber who read my manuscript and attracted my attention to many of my mistakes. Other people who helped with the book were John Abou Elias who designed the wonderful cover picture and Rudy Chidiac who contributed through his wonderful drawing "Winds of New Beginnings" for the Angels in Training program. My gratitude also goes to all of my friends and colleagues at the Seekers Of Wisdom and the Angels in Training program. Their support and devotion means the world to me.

I am also grateful to all the great teachers who passed through my life whether at school, university, or school again. Their impact on my life whether intended or not did not go unnoticed. I also thank my very supportive friends Lila Beainy and Patrick Haddad who helped me by being who they are.

Finally, I thank my family, and especially my dad, for his support whether financially or through the heated spiritual discussions we hold. Your effect on my life will never be forgotten or replaced.

May all of the people mentioned or unmentioned here be forever blessed and loved...

C.T.

The

Destined

Journey

Chapter I: The Child

The village was surging with life. The market was filled with sounds and noises of people buying, selling and bartering. Women had jugs of water upon their heads and were heading home. Every now and then, horses with chariots passed by adding on to the noise of the busy streets. Children were busily playing games near one of the houses.

I walked through the village trying to take in all that surrounded me. As I passed by the playful children, one of them caught my attention. He was about four years old with slightly tanned skin. He sat alone on the stairs leading up to the house I saw last night. I looked up to the house and saw a woman standing by the window. She was busily working on something I could not see. As I stared at her, she seemed to grow even more beautiful. The smile never left her lips as she busily worked and occasionally glanced towards the child on the stairs. Her hair was partially covered with a veil but her beauty was breathtaking.

Then, I moved my sight back to the child and was amazed by his radiant beauty. I'd never seen anything like this before. The sight of it warmed me up and I couldn't but stare. This child was definitely not of this earth. In all the people I've met on my journey, I've never seen something as beautiful and as magical as him. I just stood there and contemplated this beauty for as long as I could remember. I couldn't move my eyes away from him.

Suddenly, as if to acknowledge my presence, the child - if that's what he was - looked up towards me and smiled. Then, he gestured me with his hand to come closer. My heart was filled with joy. I hurried on and bowed near him. Being this close to him made the warmth and the radiance coming from him even more distinct and powerful. I lost myself besides this being. I couldn't think nor move anymore. There was nothing I wanted more than being right here, right now. This was what I had been looking for. This was the truth I needed.

The child put his hand on my shoulder. I lifted my head and looked up. My gaze met his eyes and he stared deeply into me. Now, I completely lost myself and felt that I had become one with him, no, one with everything. In his eyes I could see everything. I became everything. I felt true peace. Love was everywhere. He filled everything and everything was in him. What a miracle!

In his divine gaze, everything made sense. All my questions were answered and then seemed trivial. My entire journey had come to its end but I could see it again from the beginning...

Chapter II: My Guru

I had lived all my life in a small village in India. My father owned a large crop field near it where my mother and I used to help him plant rice sometimes. Of course, we were not enough and he usually had to hire workers, and especially when it was time to reap. I didn't like working in the fields but I usually did it to honor my father as it is the custom in our country.

My father wasn't wise, but I always thought that he was the innocent kind. He was always eager to help others even when they didn't ask. This, sometimes, brought him pain when some of the people he helped didn't care about what he was doing. But all in all, he never sent someone who came to him away. As for my mother, she played an important role in balancing my father's need to be constantly giving. She wasn't greedy or stingy at all, but she didn't trust people too much. My dad doesn't usually think twice about what he is giving or to who while my mom always brought some sense into him and forced him to reconsider when he was being too helpful.

I loved the region where we lived. Due to my father's work in rice plantations, we owned a lot of land around the house which insured that we were somewhat far from the next house. Everything was quiet and conducive to a healthy physical and mental life. Out of all the lands we owned, my favorite spot was always by the river. When I was young, I would go there to watch the water and the trees. I also loved to play with the frogs by the riverside. Despite our status as a wealthy family, I don't remember having had many friends when I was young. Most of my childhood memories are either of me by myself or with my parents. I didn't really care about having friends because I felt that I didn't need any. I always had something to do and somewhere to go. My parents never forbade me from going anywhere or from talking to anyone, but I always preferred to watch nature.

As I grew older, I discovered that my real love and passion was to learn. I loved to spend time at the temple in the village where an old monk lived. I fail to remember his name and I don't think he ever mentioned it because I always referred to him as "master". All I know is that I liked him maybe more than my own father. He taught me how to read and interpret the Vedas and other texts. We used to talk for hours on end. Night would fall and I would get scolded by my mother for being late but then I'd go and stay with him late the following night.

I had learned so much from my guru, especially about life. He wasn't the person who complicated things, but made them as easy as possible. He was able to express the deepest and most complex ideas in very simple words and expressions. I remember most of the conversations I had with him, but one is always more vivid than the others.

"My son, why do you think we are here?" he asked.

"To be happy," I replied surely, "this is what I learned from you."

"That is true," he nodded with a smile, "but how can we be happy?"

This was a new question for me and I hesitated before I answered.

"By doing our duty."

"What if your duty brought you sorrow?"

"What do you mean?"

"Well, you do your duty towards your father when you help him in the fields, but does that bring you happiness?"

"No, it doesn't. But it does save me a lot of sorrow and problems with my father."

"That is true. And that's the goal of duty. Duty itself does not guarantee happiness, but salvation from sorrow."

"Then what brings happiness?"

"Each person has his own journey towards happiness. No two people can follow the same route. But each person's journey is a lesson to the others."

"If that's the case, then how can one find his journey?"

"That's the real problem here," he answered thoughtfully; "some people may live their whole lives without ever knowing why they are here or what their mission is. This is actually the case with most people."

"And what happens to them?"

"I don't really know the answer yet and I'm still trying to find it. But what I know is that our journey is not very hard to find. We probably already know it but we don't realize it."

"What is your journey?"

"My journey is to teach. Whenever I talk with someone and share my knowledge with him, I become happier and I understand things I didn't know before."

"I think I understand," I replied trying to keep up, "but how did you know this?"

"Each person is born with some things that he likes to do. Some people like working in the land, others like to sail the seas, and others may like to teach. It is in these talents that we find our true journey. What do you like to do?"

"I like to learn as much as I can. I find my true pleasure in studying the holy texts for example."

"I feel that this is not all you like, there is something else. I know that you have many dreams."

"Well yes, I would like to travel and see what lies beyond the horizons."

"And that is most probably where your journey lies."

"You mean that I should travel?"

"What I am saying is that you should think about what your dream is and how you will realize it."

"But if I am to travel, what will become of my parents?"

"Your parents are pious people and they understand what it is to have faith in the Lord."

"I see."

"Yes, the Lord will not forsake them. An apple that stays in its mother tree will not become a tree itself. The apple cannot grow into a tree unless it leaves its mother tree and set on its own journey to find the place where it can grow and prosper."

"But, if I am to leave, where will I go?"

"You will know. Have patience, stay open-minded and all your answers will come to you."

"But when?"

"Nothing happens unless it's the right time for it to happen. Trust the Lord and know that His will will be done when it should be done."

"I will do that."

I meditated for some time besides my guru and then decided to go back home. On my way, I couldn't stop thinking about his words. He was right and now I knew what I had to wait for. I had faith that I would be getting a sign soon.

I couldn't sleep that night and I didn't want to sleep. The words of my guru kept turning in my head without a rest. On the next morning, I woke up early and headed to the fields to help my dad. There was nothing specifically odd about that day and everything went on smoothly as we reaped the crops.

Chapter III: The First Sign

The rice of my father's fields was of a very good quality, as I always heard customers say. We had many regular customers who would show up every now and then to inquire about the state and the current price. My dad didn't charge too much although he had every right to do so. He always felt that he shouldn't be greedy and always worked to keep his conscience clear.

It was in the late afternoon when someone showed up by the field. He was wearing clothes made of white silk and a green turban. The man was not one of our regular customers. His yellowish skin and his almond-shaped eyes suggested that he was Chinese. He greeted us and seemed to speak our language fluently.

"Good day," he said, "who owns these lands?"

"I do," replied my father with a welcoming smile, "how may I help you?"

"My name is Hao Chan. I come from the land of Yutian," he introduced himself; "I am looking for rice."

"Why did you come here?" asked my father in surprise, "China has plenty of rice."

"This seems to be an unlucky year," answered Hao Chan, "our fields did not yield enough crops and we are looking to buy rice from here."

"That's terrible," exclaimed my father, "the rice season here in India seems to be pretty abundant."

"That's why I'm here. My patron sent me to buy as much rice as I could from India."

"And I assume you want to buy some of my rice."

"All of it actually. And I have plenty of gold to pay you. The people in the area recommended your rice over many other people's crops. However, there is one small problem."

"Which is?"

"I need your help in transporting them because my crew was ambushed on our way here and the bandits took everything. Most of my crewmembers died and the others left back to Yutian."

"You are one unlucky man!"

"Not at all, as long as I have my two legs and the capacity to go on, I will keep doing my patron's work."

"Very well. Let us see what we can do about your situation."

"Yes, can you come with me?" asked Hao Chan enthusiastically, "You know the lands better than I."

"I cannot leave my family. I am trying to think of someone who may be able to go with you. I assume you know the roads better than us when you are in China, no?"

"That is true. But who do you have in mind and who is trustworthy enough to accompany me?"

That was my sign. This was my chance to finally start my journey and to find my happiness.

"I will go," I interjected, "I can take you."

"What?" asked my father surprised, "you want to go with him?"

"Yes father," I replied, "I ask your permission to accompany him."

"Let's discuss this with your mother when we get back home," replied my father, "we will see what we can do."

"Well then," said Hao Chan, "I will meet you back here tomorrow morning so that we finalize our deal."

"But you must stay for dinner tonight!" added my father, "wouldn't you like to try the rice first?"

"No," replied Hao Chan smiling, "there is no need for that and I also have a lot of business to attend to at the moment."

Hao Chan bowed and left the fields. I finished what I was doing and ran to the temple as fast as I could. I needed to tell my guru about this. I pushed the temple door open and entered. My guru was in a deep meditation but he opened his eyes and smiled when he heard the door opening.

"I feel that you have something important to tell me," he said with his peaceful smile, "go ahead."

I told him all about the man and his proposal and asked his advice regarding what I should do.

"It seems that your journey is about to begin. Good luck and may you never forget that the Lord is beside you."

"I will always remember that. However, I need your advice on something else."

"Yes?"

"I'm thinking of not only stopping at Yutian. I want to continue my journey from there, but I don't know how."

"Simple, just wait and follow the signs."

"How will I know the signs?"

"They will come when you need them most. Just like the man who came out of the blue with his proposal, many others will come with other proposals. Just go with the flow. Remember to stay vigilant. And this is what I should talk to you about before you leave."

"What?"

"Observation. Your journey should be a mixture of two things: observation and seizing your chance. You have to be aware of all what is happening around you and never disregard something as pure hazard. Listen and observe all that happens until you receive the sign you need to continue your journey. As soon as you receive that information, seize it and continue your way."

"But what if I miss it?"

"Don't worry, many other signs will show up; however, they will not be as good as the first one. So, always remain vigilant and observing."

"I will do this. Is there anything else I should know before I leave?"

"Tell your parents of your intention to start your journey. And I will be with you in my thoughts and my love for you."

"I will. Thank you for being my guru."

"Thank you for giving me the chance to learn from you," he concluded with a smile I never forgot.

As I left the temple that evening, I was both happy and sad. I knew that I will miss my guru more than anyone else. But I was happy that I will finally start on my journey. I went back home. My parents were busily discussing the man's proposal as I entered the house. They seemed to be happy about it a lot. When they noticed me, my father informed me that they had both agreed on my travelling with the man. I informed them of my choice that I want to continue travelling even after I'm done helping the man. They were both shocked. A tear came to my mother's eye.

"So soon?" asked my father as he put his hand on my shoulder, "We both knew that you will come to this decision one day We have always seen your free soul and your spirit starving for knowledge and wisdom. You are a grown man now. We cannot hold you back. Our prayers will be with you wherever you go."

"But please," added my mother still crying, "write for us from wherever you are so that we know that you are safe."

"Don't worry mother. I will always write for you and will never forget what good parents you were to me. I love you both very much."

That night, I had to force myself to sleep even though my mind was surging with thoughts about the journey which lay ahead of me. In order to fall asleep, I started listing the things I will need to pack in my mind. I needed clothes, washing material, some books, and of course some writing materials. There were many other things I needed to think of but, no matter what, my mind would always drift back to the idea of the journey. I just couldn't get it out of my head.

Chapter IV: My Journey Begins

The next morning, I was the first to wake up and head to the fields. The sun was barely up and I knew that I was probably early, as usual, and I'd have to wait for a long time for Hao Chan to come. I just went there and decided to meditate for a while and try to clear my mind. Some time through my mostly useless meditation, I heard some footsteps. I opened my eyes and turned around to see Hao Chan coming up behind me. I stood up and went towards him. He shook my hands and greeted me with a smile.

"You're up early, I see," he said humorously.

"I know," I replied, "I couldn't sleep. And you're also early, right?"

"I always come early," he answered, "If there's something that I detest, it's being late to anything."

"Well," I replied with a laugh, "sit down for a bit, my dad is late sometimes."

"Not today," he answered surely as he pointed to a figure approaching us.

It was my father. He approached us and shook Hao Chan's hand.

"I assume your answer is a positive one," Said Hao Chan happily.

"Yes," nodded my father, "It is. My son will be accompanying you and showing you the way."

"I am extremely grateful," replied Hao Chan, "my patron will be so happy and will reward you handsomely."

"How will you be transporting the rice to Yutian?" asked my father.

"I was informed that my patron has sent me some gold. Most of it is yours and, with the rest, I will purchase a wagon and some rations for our travel."

"That is good. When will you be leaving?"

"Tonight. I need to hurry back to Yutian. I've already lost enough time and my people are starving to death."

"Very well," replied my father, "I will have all the rice bags ready and waiting for your wagon."

"And I will prepare myself and get some sleep," I added, "I will be ready as soon as you come."

"Excellent news," exclaimed Hao Chan happily, "I will have your gold ready tonight as well."

Who was I trying to fool? I could barely sleep all day but at least I rested for a bit so that I'd have enough energy to help out when night came.

I could see the sun setting from my bedroom window. When it became totally dark, I got out of my bed and changed my clothes. In the meantime, my mother had prepared some bags full of clean clothes for my journey and a big meal for the family. It was her way of bidding me farewell. The three of us sat down for dinner. My mother was smiling but I could sense her pain. I wished that I could ease it for her but I had to do this. My father was a bit sad but very happy, not because of the money, but because he was seeing me as a grown man now and not a child.

When we finished our dinner, I went back to my room, chose some of my favorite books and stored them carefully in my bags, in addition to some papers and writing materials. Then, I went to the field. My father had his workmen gather all the bags of rice in one of the barns and locked it. When we got there, we saw that Hao Chan and his wagon were already there and waiting. It was one of the biggest wagons I've ever seen. Six horses were tied to it and waiting to pull it. Hao Chan was standing by it and greeted us when he saw us. Then, he went to the back, opened the wagon and brought out a large bag which made a clinking sound as it fell to the ground. It was full of gold.

"All of this is yours," announced Hao Chan to my father.

"Thank you my friend," replied my father, "I never expected that much. You and your patron are very generous."

"Yes, my patron is a very good man."

"Let's start packing, shall we?"

"Yes, of course. The wagon is open and I will help you load the rice in it. After that, my little friend and I will put our bags in the back along with the tent and the food that I have ready."

My father opened the barn and Hao Chan smiled when he saw the rice. We quickly moved the bags into the wagon which could barely support the weight. Then, Hao Chan and I put our bags in the back and he closed the wagon. By the time we were done, we were sweaty and hungry. That's when my mother showed up and called us for supper. Hao Chan tried to insist on leaving straight away but the prospect of a hot, homemade supper and a warm shower were too tempting that he couldn't refuse.

We went back to the home and had supper together. After that, Hao Chan and I washed one after the other which allowed us to get some rest before departing. Finally, we were ready to go. We headed back to the wagon. Hao Chan took the Wagoner's seat and waited for me to take my seat beside him. Meanwhile, my father called me aside and shoved a bag full of gold into my hands.

"These are for you," he said, "They might come in handy on your way in case you need to buy something."

I thanked him and then climbed the wagon and sat beside Hao Chan. He called after the horses and struck them with his whip till they started moving and pulling the wagon. And we were on our way through the night. With every turn of the wheels, my heart swelled with joy more and more.

For the first hour or so, none of us spoke a word. The night was silent and all that was disturbing the silence was the sound of the wheels and the horses' hooves clicking against the stony road. This whole setting made me feel rather sleepy. It seemed that Hao Chan sensed this and so, broke the silence.

"So, what is your name?" he asked.

"I'm Vishnu."

"Nice name, the name of your savior god."

"How did you know that? Are you Hindu too?"

"No my friend, I'm simply a spiritual person, like my patron, with a vast knowledge of most religions in the neighboring kingdoms."

"What do you mean by spiritual?"

"It simply means that I don't define my god with a name or a shape. I simply choose to believe in his existence and surrender myself to his will."

"I see. This is the same as in the Hindu religion regarding devotion to a god."

"This is practically the case in most religions, not just the Hindu religion. What differs is simply the name that each religion gives to this divinity or this power which is causing everything."

"You sound like my guru."

"The one in the temple of your village?"

"Yes, him. Have you met him?"

"Of course. And I've had a wonderful discussion with him. A very wise man indeed."

This journey seemed to be off to a good start. Not an hour had passed before I already started discovering new insights into God. I started feeling more at ease and knew that I was on the right track.

"What are you thinking of?" asked Hao Chan and interrupted the silence of my thoughts.

"I'm just remembering something my guru told me."

"Would you mind telling me about it?"

"Sure, why not. He was the prime reason for my coming on this trip with you. We were talking about how each person has a mission and a destiny to follow."

"I see. And what is your mission?"

"To travel and learn as much as I could about the Lord."

"A worthy goal indeed. I hope you will be able to persevere till the end."

"Are you on a mission as well?"

"My only purpose is to serve my patron with all myself."

"Why? Why aren't you on a mission for yourself?"

"My patron's goals are my own and therefore, I trust in him."

"I see. What are your patron's goals?"

"He wishes to make life in Yutian more spiritual and more pleasant. He and his people live there in a spiritual and wise way."

"That is very interesting."

"Indeed. And how is he faring?"

"Pretty well. All would've been better were it not for the bad crops. But my patron has faith. He believes that this is also for the good of the town."

"Why is your patron doing this? What's in it for him?"

"You see, the goal is not and should not be selfish. It is for everyone. His ultimate goal is to show the world that there can be peace if we live in a spiritual, non-religious way."

"What is your patron's name anyway?"

"Liu Shang. He used to be a very rich merchant but then bought the land in Yutian to build his peaceful kingdom."

"I am eager to see what he has done when we arrive."

"I bet my patron would be very happy to meet you and to show you around himself."

From then on, our journey went uneventfully. Hao Chan was an excellent travel mate from whom I learned a lot about some very important things and especially devotion and selflessness. His love for his patron and their selfless goal was unmatched. He made me reevaluate all my goals and the purpose of my journey. I learned that it was for my own satisfaction and my own self-gratification. My journey didn't change. I couldn't change it; however, I didn't know what I am to do now.

"I've been thinking about what you said," I told him once.

"Yes?"

"I think that maybe I should get back home as soon as we get the rice to Yutian."

"Why is that? I thought you wanted to travel even further."

"I am doing this for me not for someone else."

"And?"

"The Vedas taught me over and over again that I should be selfless and that I should be devoted to someone. But in this journey, all I'm doing is pleasing myself. I left my parents, brokenhearted, behind me and I just went on my own."

"Calm down my friend. Not all journeys start selflessly. So far, all you know from your journey is the first checkpoint, which is Yutian. Who knows what will happen after this? Who knows what will happen when we get there?"

"Are you saying that I should go on?"

"I am saying that you should be patient and observe the circumstances. Your journey, as you said, started with the sign which was my proposal. So it started with a sign, which is how all journeys should start. So far, all's been going well."

"But why am I having doubts now? Isn't that a sign too? I know intuition is a sign."

"You're not having intuition; you are having worries and fears. These weigh you down and make you believe that you are doing the wrong thing. My advice is to keep an eye on your roots, which is how your journey started, and another eye on your closest objective, which is reaching Yutian. That way, you will be able to vanquish your fears and stay focused."

"Then that's what I'll do. I'm really glad to be alongside you. I'm learning a lot from you."

"A truly spiritual person never hides or keeps information to himself."

"You've learned all this from your patron?"

"Not at all. I've learned most of this myself but my patron helped me find the connections."

We travelled in the wagon for months during which Hao Chan taught me his language since I would need it on the way. When we were near a village, we would stay at an inn there. At other times, we would camp as soon as we found a good place, safe from wild beasts. Two days before our arrival, Hao Chan started feeling odd. He didn't know the reason he was feeling thus, but knew that there was something wrong. He felt sicker and sicker the closer we got to Yutian. That's when his feelings proved right.

Chapter V: Yutian

We arrived to Yutian, but it was not the glorious city that I conceived in my imagination based on Hao Chan's description of it. Yutian seemed to have been a victim of a recent catastrophe by the look of things. Most of the buildings were destroyed; others bore the signs of a fire having burned them and charred what remained of them.

"Oh my God!" exclaimed Hao Chan with tears in his eyes, "What happened here?"

"There seems to have been a battle!" I replied.

"The Luciferic powers took control again."

"The what?"

"We must go find my patron. He will explain everything."

I followed Hao Chan through the ravaged city streets. None of the buildings seemed to have survived the battle. Also, there were no people in sight. The streets were empty and nothing stirred. Hao Chan led the way to one of the buildings. Like the others, it bore the same marks of chaos haunting the city. The only difference however, was the light coming out through the window. There was someone inside with a fire lit. Hao Chan knocked on the door and pushed it open. I followed him inside.

We entered into a room with a soft fire burning in its middle. The whole room was in a chaotic state. The windows were broken as well as the furniture and everything else. Nothing seemed to have escaped the destruction. In the room also, sitting on the floor with his head between his knees and rocking to and fro, there was a man. He didn't look up towards us as we came in.

"Liu Shang!" called Hao Chan, "is that you?"

"Hao?" replied the man, "I'm so sorry!"

When he looked up at us, I could see his face clearly, even though it looked like it hadn't been washed in some time. Liu Shang had Hao Chan's same almond-shaped eyes. His skin was somewhat paler but his face looked more authoritative, although somewhat broken.

"What happened? How did the Luciferic forces come here?"

"It's all my fault!" Contemplated Liu Shang morosely, "I should've stopped them."

"Please master, calm down and explain!"

"Despite the food crisis, everything was going well. I was in charge of distributing the little food we had, but all was going well. Everyone was satisfied. Then, we got the news of your small mishap. After we sent you the money, they started fearing that there will not be enough food until you come back. So, they thought that we should institutionalize things and distribute the rations equally to each person."

"So, the Ahrimanic forces set in first?"

"Exactly. I tried to resist them but they were too many. They simply shoved me aside and did things their way. Almost everyone was happy, until the resources started dwindling. The rations became smaller and smaller until they were only enough for those in charge of the distribution."

"And I assume that's when the Luciferic forces showed up."

"Yes, the people couldn't take this anymore and so started the rebellion. Many were killed, everything was destroyed, and everyone left. Everyone except me."

"Stop blaming yourself master…"

"Stop calling me master, I'm worthless," shouted Liu Shang, "I couldn't do anything to stop it."

"Exactly, you could not do anything to stop it. It was out of your hands. Now get back on your feet and let's set things straight."

"But we can't do it alone."

"We'll figure things out. Don't worry; I will not leave your side."

"You're a wonderful friend Hao. Thanks for all you're doing for me."

"It's my duty, master."

"Why do you still insist on calling me master?"

"Well, you've taught me so much that I consider myself your disciple. There is nothing that can change that."

"Who's you're friend?"

"That's Vishnu. He accompanied me here all the way from India."

"Vishnu!" said Liu Shang with a giggle, "the savior. There is nothing left to save though!"

"It's an honor to meet you, master," I said, "Hao Chan spoke very highly of you and I am eager to learn what I can from you."

"I see. And what do you expect to learn from me?"

"First of all, I want to understand all this Luciferic and Ahrimanic forces talk."

"Very well. I will talk about these with you over dinner. I assume you brought the rice Hao Chan."

"They are in the wagon," answered Hao Chan, "where shall we unload them?"

"I think the storage rooms are still in a good enough shape, we should put them there."

"Very well, let's go."

Hao Chan brought the wagon while Liu Shang and I met him at the storage rooms. They were somehow in a better shape than the other buildings. They were charred from the outside, but the walls were still firmly in place. The three of us unloaded the rice into the storage rooms and Liu Shang locked the doors in the end. By the time we were done, it was already evening and we were very tired and hungry. We went back to Liu Shang's home and took our shower. Liu Shang went first but only to be able to cook a dinner during the time we were washing up. Finally, we sat together and had a well deserved dinner.

"So, you want to know about the Luciferic and Ahrimanic forces," started Liu Shang as we ate.

"Of course I do," I answered, "you seem to attach a lot of importance to them."

"Very well then, listen. There are three forces controlling the world: Ahrimanic, Luciferic, and Angelic. The Ahrimanic and Luciferic forces are opposites. They are both named after some of the gods of neighboring kingdoms and peoples. But keep in mind; I do not believe that these gods are more than ideas. I believe that there is only one god and he is all there is and all there will ever be."

"That's the same as what I, as a Hindu, believe. We have one God who is Brahma, and all other gods are different faces of him."

"That is true. But unfortunately, people start to attach more importance to the faces than the actual God. Now, back to Ahriman and Lucifer. Ahriman is the god of order. He represents extreme order. He wants everything to be planned, repetitive and systematic. He is an obsession with order. Whereas, Lucifer represents the complete opposite: the extreme obsession with chaos. He wants everything to be unplanned and chaotic."

"What about the Angelic forces?"

"Be patient, I'm getting there. The Luciferic and Ahrimanic forces possess people from time to time, as you have certainly understood from what happened here. These forces are always there and waiting to be released."

"What triggers them?"

"Fear, of course, since it is the source of all other negative emotions. When the people feared starving to death, the Ahrimanic forces were released. As soon as these forces took root in the people, the natural tendency towards balance was set in action. The only force able to balance Ahrimanic forces is Luciferic. And so, the battle starts between both thus sending the world to destruction. And that's why there are Angelic forces."

"So basically, Ahrimanic and Luciferic forces can take control of people when fear sets in. How?"

"Well, every person has all three forces inside of him, but they are usually balanced. When there is fear, depending on the situation, either of the Ahrimanic or the Luciferic forces take over."

"I see. Now what about the Angelic forces?"

"The Angelic forces are what keeps the Ahrimanic and Luciferic forces balanced and dormant. A person who is strong and unafraid is under the influence of Angelic forces. As soon as he is afraid, one of the others takes over and an inner battle begins."

"But what happened here wasn't an inner battle."

"No, it wasn't. When the same fear is in more than one person, these people have a tendency to gather and attract one another. Thus, the force becomes stronger and more powerful. Then, it translates itself physically in wars and rebellions."

"That's making sense. But what do the Angelic forces really do?"

"They guide you and provide you with intuitions. They are the prime force driving us on our destined paths in life."

"How?"

"Easy, the more you are on your path, the stronger the Angelic forces are in you. When you have fears and doubts, one of the other forces manifests itself."

"Which is what started to happen with me on our way here. Were it not for Hao Chan, I would've done my job and gone back home instead of staying with you. But which force took over me?"

"It was the Ahrimanic forces," answered Hao Chan, "you wanted to get back to your systematic and repetitive life."

"Now I understand," I replied, "but how were you able to quiet it down?"

"You see," answered Hao Chan, "just like Ahrimanic forces attract Ahrimanic forces and Luciferic forces attract Luciferic forces, Angelic forces also attract Angelic forces. The Angelic forces in you were what attracted me to you in the rice fields. And since both of us had the same force in us, I was able to quiet you down when I sensed one of the other forces taking over."

"So that's how the signs are generated!" I exclaimed.

"Exactly," explained Liu Shang, "a sign is generated when two people with angelic forces meet. At least one of them has to be aware of these forces in order to recognize it in the other. Knowing the effect of all three forces, a person with an Angelic force can help another person maintain a level of Angelic forces within him."

"But what if no one knew the effect of the forces?"

"The same thing as what happened here happens."

"But you knew about them!"

"I know, but I was alone and I couldn't quiet down everyone. The level of Angelic forces within me was unable to calm down the surge of Ahrimanic forces in all the others and so, the Ahrimanic forces took over."

"That's a very big problem. No Angelic person can stand against a whole army of Ahrimanic or Luciferic people."

"Actually, there are a few who were able to do it. They were the great leaders that everyone knows. Even though they may not have known about the forces, they were able to work with them well."

"It is rare to find someone like this though," I interrupted.

"True. That's why people with Angelic forces should stick together. Otherwise, they will not be of much use. It's a good thing that the forces attract forces like them and we should use this fact to our advantage."

"How?"

"We keep empowering each other and reminding each other of the Angelic forces within us. Otherwise, when fear shows up, we will not have time to think about them and we'll surrender to Ahrimanic or Luciferic forces."

"There's one more thing I want to know."

"Ask away."

"Luciferic forces are related to Lucifer and Ahrimanic forces are related to Ahriman. Are Angelic forces related to Angels?"

"Just like Lucifer and Ahriman are ideas, so are angels. We are the angels when we awaken and empower the Angelic forces within us."

We continued our discussions deep into the night. When the fire started to die out, we were already too tired and sleepy that we fell asleep one after the other. I also learned that the word "angel" comes from Latin and means "messenger", which is what we become when the Angelic forces within us empower the Angelic forces in others.

Chapter VI: The Second Sign

I woke up late in the morning on the next day. Liu Shang and Hao Chan were up before me and were nowhere in sight. I raised myself from my sleepy position and stood up slowly, still thinking about last evening's discussion. I went to the bathroom and washed my face, then headed back towards the living room where we had been sleeping on the floor wrapped in some thick covers. There was still some food left from last evening so I ate some of it for breakfast and went outside to search for the others. They were nowhere in sight so I just walked around the old city streets looking for them. As I strolled on, I started hearing whispers so I followed them. They started getting louder and louder until I could hear my companion's voices distinctly. However, there was an additional third voice. I went closer and closer until they were in sight. Hao Chan heard me coming, turned towards me and called me to come closer.

"This is Feroz, he's a messenger from King Gaspar," started Hao Chan, "He has just arrived from Jenikand in the west."

"A pleasure meeting you Feroz," I replied as I shook his hand, "My name is Vishnu and I came from India."

"The pleasure is all mine, Vishnu," he replied with a gentle smile, "anyway Liu Shang, I was telling you that King Gaspar has heard of what happened here and would like you to go visit him before you start any repairs."

"That seems like a good idea now," answered Liu Shang, "I'll discuss it with my companions and see about it. Meanwhile, you are more than welcome to spend as much time as you like in what remains of Yutian."

"I am grateful for your hospitality," replied Feroz, "I accept it gladly and hope that I will not be lonely on my way back to Jenikand."

We walked back to Liu Shang's house with Feroz. Liu Shang heated up the food for him and then called us to the adjoining room to discuss. I had already made up my mind and wanted to go to Jenikand with or without them, but I hoped that they would join me.

"So my friends, what do you think?" asked Liu Shang.

"I am going with Feroz," I announced surely.

"Why so sure?" asked Liu Shang.

"It's part of his journey," replied Hao Chan, "he wants to travel and learn more spiritual truths."

"I see," exclaimed Liu Shang, "then Jenikand is the best place for you to go. King Gaspar is a very wise man and is eager to share his wisdom with all those who would listen."

"But what about you two?" I asked.

"Master," said Hao Chan, "I believe we should accompany them. First, the road is too long for them and second, if King Gaspar has sent you an invitation, it means that he has discovered something new and of importance to you."

"You are right," replied Liu Shang, "but what am I to do with the city here?"

"Just leave it," answered Hao Chan, "there is nothing worthwhile in it anyway and all you'll be getting from this is more depression. I suggest you move on."

"I guess you're right," replied Liu Shang, "then I believe that's settled. We will be leaving as soon as we are ready."

We went back to Feroz and informed him of our decision. He was very happy at the prospect of having three companions on his long road which, as I was informed, would take more than three months. After he rested from his travel, Feroz helped us pack some food and some clothes in addition to the tent into the wagon. The next morning, we were all ready and set off on our new journey to Jenikand.

Feroz was only a messenger and didn't have much of importance to say. All he liked talking about were the horses and the places he visited. As I could understand from him, he was a loyal servant and messenger for King Gaspar and he would travel anywhere for him. I also learned that King Gaspar was Liu Shang's teacher but they didn't meet in more than ten years.

"Gaspar," told us Liu Shang, "before he became king, was an astrologer. I guess that he is still one now because astrology runs in his blood."

"Yes," affirmed Feroz, "he hasn't changed a bit."

"Does he still trust everything based on the stars?"

"Yes he does. However, I did notice a change in him during the last days before he sent me to you."

"He probably foresaw the rebellion in Yutian."

"Why didn't you stay with Gaspar?" I asked.

"Gaspar is more of an observer; I am more of a doer. He believes, that - because of the Luciferic and Ahrimanic powers - peace is not an option on earth. Meanwhile, I believed that, if we lived consciously, we could reach true peace. That's why I set out to build Yutian. He funded most of my endeavors although he knew that they were doomed to failure."

"Why is that?"

"I don't know. But, from my knowledge of Gaspar, he probably saw something in it for me and that's why he let me do it. Otherwise, he wouldn't have helped me."

"Something like what?" I asked in surprise, "Yutian has been demolished."

"Gaspar never attached any importance to material wealth. What I meant is that he probably thought that I'd learn a lesson from what I am doing, or perhaps I'd meet someone or maybe I'd be of use to someone. Who knows?"

"He seems to be a very mysterious man, though."

"Believe me, he is. I still can't quite explain most of the things he used to say or do."

Chapter VII: The Astrologer

With the three companions by my side, the three months of the journey went by quickly. Soon enough, we were already making our way through the city streets toward King Gaspar's observatory. When we got there, there was someone waiting for us at the door.

"There is Gaspar already waiting for us," exclaimed Liu Shang.

"Yes, that's him," replied Feroz as the wagon arrived to a halt in front of him and the four of us jumped off.

"Welcome my friends;" shouted the king with a beaming smile in Chinese although he wasn't Chinese himself, "I expected your arrival."

King Gaspar wasn't much older than Liu Shang. This was apparent through his posture and graceful movements. However, his long beard and unkempt attire in general made him look older than he really was.

"Your stars told you, I guess," joked Liu Shang as he gave Gaspar a friendly hug.

"I'm so sorry for your misfortune old friend," apologized Gaspar, "It had to happen."

"But why?"

"I'll explain once we are inside. You have to introduce me to your friends first!"

"These are Hao Chan, my trusty advisor and friend and Vishnu, our dear companion on the search for spiritual knowledge."

"A seeker, I see," said Gaspar as he gave me a look which seemed to pierce into my soul, "then we'll have a lot to share."

"I will be honored to learn from you," I replied hesitantly, "Liu Shang spoke very highly of your wisdom."

"Cut the cordiality," he said with a laugh, "I will learn from our discussions more than you will ever learn from me."

"You sound so much like my guru back in India."

"Who said that I'm not?" He concluded with a knowing smirk and opened the door for us to enter his observatory.

We entered King Gaspar's observatory which was both an observatory and a study. By the look of it, it seemed that Gaspar never needed to leave this place since everything he needs was in here. The observatory was made of two floors. On the ground floor, there was an office and a library full of books and maps of the stars, the kingdom and other kingdoms. As for the second floor, it was a big room with no windows but with an opening in the ceiling. The opening was just like a window and could be closed in case of rain or snow. In the room there was also a table with many scrolls of paper on it and a stack of different sized parchments. In addition to all this, there was a tall ladder in the room which, I believe, Gaspar uses to climb up to the hatch in the ceiling. When we got to the second floor, Gaspar cleared the table from all his papers and tools and put them aside neatly on a smaller table. Then, he called to his cook and told him to bring food. Meanwhile, he asked us to sit and rest from our journey.

"I believe Liu Shang already explained to you about the Luciferic, Ahrimanic and Angelic forces," started Gaspar.

"Yes he has," I answered, "I find this very interesting."

"Then let me tell you a bit about astrology. It's what I do here. There are as many interpretations of the stars as there are astrologers. No two astrologers agree on everything totally. And that's why astrology is an interesting study."

"But if it's not sure, how can it be counted on?"

"It doesn't matter whether it's right or wrong, what really matters is what you make of it."

"I don't understand," I said sheepishly.

"What I'm trying to say is that what you make out of your own astrological reading is what you need to learn and understand. It doesn't matter whether it actually is right or wrong."

"But isn't astrology supposed to tell you about your future?"

"No my friend, the future is not written in the stars, nor anywhere else for that matter. Reading the stars is seeing the present from a different perspective."

"I am starting to understand."

"Good! The universe is like a giant mind which records everything. Whatever happens, then, is recorded in the universe. Astrologers are the people who can read that book; however, they do not choose which page they open. But, they know that whichever page is chosen for them, there is information inside it which they need to learn."

"That sounds very similar to our I-Ching," interrupted Liu Shang, "it's a book of prophecies. We flip some coins for a few times and they lead us to the page containing the information we need."

"All divination methods are similar and all are trustworthy, provided you know why you are using them!" answered Gaspar, "Always remember that you are using them to understand your present and never to foresee your future."

"But how did you know about the rebellion in Yutian?" asked Liu Shang.

"You don't need astrology to know that," explained Gaspar, "It was simply based on my observation of the forces of Ahriman and Lucifer. I received news regarding the failure of the rice crops there and I just guessed the time your people would need until the Ahrimanic forces took control. And that's how I somehow predicted the future. I could've been completely wrong though."

"The strange operations of your mind never cease to amaze me Gaspar," laughed Liu Shang, "you're one of a kind."

"So are you my friend," replied Gaspar as he turned back to me, "where was I?"

"You were telling me about using divination to get a different perspective on your present."

"Oh yes. I believe you already know that everyone is on a journey."

"Yes. I am on my own journey too."

"That's good. Sometimes, you reach a place in your journey when you don't know where you should go or what you should do and no new signs seem to be showing up. That's when you turn to astrology or divination."

"And will it help?"

"It depends on what you make of them. If you decide to work upon their indications, you will not fail, although sometimes you may seem to have failed."

"What do you mean?"

"Sometimes, if you work based on divination, you may find yourself in a lot of trouble. This is what makes most people lose faith in divination. However, for someone who is spiritual, it will be clear that these problems aren't problems, but learning opportunities."

"So even when you fail, you don't really fail?"

"You can ask our friend Liu Shang here! His endeavors to make a peaceful community ended in failure, haven't they?"

"Yes they have," answered Liu Shang, "but I don't see what good came out of them!"

"Before now," answered Gaspar, "did you know anything about what we are talking about concerning astrology?"

"Well no," replied Liu Shang, 'but I still don't get what you're pointing at."

"If Yutian didn't get destroyed," explained Gaspar, "would you have been able to leave it and come here if I had asked you for a meeting?"

"Of course not," replied Liu Shang, "now I get your point."

"Another benefit of this was for you to bring Hao Chan here," added Gaspar.

"Me?" exclaimed Hao Chan surprised, "what does all this have to do with me?"

"We will get there soon enough my friend," answered Gaspar, "now back to our main topic. Where were we again?"

King Gaspar seemed to always have a lot on his mind. Perhaps he was thinking too fast or was preoccupied with something else. I could see this through his eyes which looked wild and unfocused as he explained things which were deep.

"We were talking about failure," I answered.

"Oh yes. In order to really learn from your mistakes or bad experiences, you should have unshakable faith in your journey. You should trust God, the universe or whatever you decided to believe in everything and never forget that because, as soon as this notion is out of your mind, Luciferic and Ahrimanic forces can take over you and then you'd be in real trouble."

"May the Lord's will be done!"

"Yes. That is the best attitude towards things. Simply make your choices based on your present circumstances and your signs or divination reading and leave the rest up to God and the Angelic forces within you."

"That makes things a lot easier."

"When you know what astrology is really for, you can start using it effectively. If you still believe that anyone can somehow tap into the universe and predict any future, except by analyzing the present, you are as misguided as the swindler who is predicting your future. My friend, you are the only one capable of walking your path."

"There seems to be a contradiction here. If you say that the future is not written somewhere, then how come there is a path?"

"The path is not a physical road that you have to tread on. It is a mixture of places you have to be in, people you have to meet and things you have to do. In addition to this, it's how your soul unfolds to understand the divine."

"This somehow reminds me of the concept of Karma."

"Do share!"

"For us Hindus, we believe in reincarnation. If you do bad deeds, you incur Karma while if you do good deeds, you get rid of some Karma."

"Yes, I've heard of this concept but I see it in a different way. I personally do not believe that we reincarnate into different bodies."

"Then how do you see it?"

"A human being is made of three parts: body, mind, and spirit. The body is the carrier of the other two and has no memory of its own. The mind however, remembers some of the things that happened and tries to analyze the present in order to work with it and adapt effectively. As for the spirit, it is a part of the universe which animates the body and the mind. Its memory is infinite, just like the universal memory and it is carried on over different lives. And this is where karma is located."

"So you believe that Karma is just located in the spirit and has nothing to do with the body or the mind?"

"No, it has a lot to do with them; however, what really gets reincarnated is neither the body nor the mind with its early memory. Only the spirit and its Karma reincarnate. So in fact, when you get a new body, you also get a new mind with a blank memory. Then, the Karma which is in the spirit acts upon the body and the mind to shape them and animate them as needed."

"But why should a new body and a new mind get old Karma. I mean, Karma is bad."

"No it's not. Karma is the work you have to accomplish. Everyone is born with an amount of Karma that he has to finish. If all the Karma in the world is finished, we will only then know true peace. However, by not following the path and by not accomplishing their journeys, people create more Karma than they finish. And this is why Karma received its negative denomination."

"That's astounding," interrupted Liu Shang, "that's why I was unable to maintain peace in Yutian!"

"Exactly," replied Gaspar, "you tried, unconsciously, to run away from Karma. But Karma found its way back to you and made you do it. So Karma will keep trying to finish itself through us no matter where we go or in what body we may be."

"And what can we do about it?" I asked.

"Enjoy it," answered Gaspar, "just work with it happily and you will see that it will treat you the same. If you work with Karma, it will work with you and make your life easier. Karma is like a river flowing through us: we can swim with it or against it. If we swim with the current it's generating, we get to where we are supposed to be easily. However, if we try to swim against the current by trying to escape Karma, our road will be tough and we will receive many blows, just like the waves which will splash in our face and send us tumbling downwards."

"I understand," I said in barely a whisper, "Karma is what we have to do. We can do it willingly or forcefully.

If we intend to work with it, it will be easy but if we try to run away from it, it will keep haunting us till we face it, and thus, it will appear bigger and more painful."

"Exactly," applauded King Gaspar, "Let's take a break now."

At that moment, the cook opened the door and started to set our table before going out to bring some food. I didn't know what I was eating and I didn't care to ask. All I knew was that it was delicious.

"What were you going to tell me?" asked Hao Chan as we were eating.

"Oh yes. I have a friend called Larvandad and he is the ruler of the city of Lansura," explained Gaspar, "a few days ago, he sent me a letter informing me of a new discovery he made. He told me that I would be very interested in it but he was sorry that he could not elaborate in the letter in fear of having it fall into the wrong hands. I have to go there but I find no one worthy enough to take over my place while I'm away.

And I know that you are faithful enough to keep order until I'm back."

"Are you serious?" inquired Hao Chan shocked, "but I've never been in charge before. How do you know that I will not destroy what you have established?"

"Calm down my friend," answered Gaspar with his gentle smile, "don't let the Luciferic powers take over you. From my regular communications with Liu Shang, I know that you are a very trustworthy person."

"Yes he is," added Liu Shang, "you can choose no better person than Hao Chan for the job."

"But," protested Hao Chan, "my master has more experience in this field, why doesn't he take over for now?"

"Because I need your master to come with me on my journey, as well as our friend Vishnu here," replied Gaspar.

"Then I will be alone here?"

"No. Don't worry. Feroz will be more than enough help for you. I trust your long trip here made you better acquaintances, no?"

"Very well then, may the Lord's will be done."

"Nice thinking, that's the best attitude to get things done. We will be leaving in a week. During this time, I will tell you about everything which must be done during my absence. And Feroz, I don't need to remind you to be always vigilant as the eyes and ears of Hao Chan in the city. He will not be going out much but you will."

"You have nothing to fear, my king," replied Feroz, "I will treat him as I would treat you."

"Thank you Feroz," replied Gaspar as he turned back to us, "now let me show you to your quarters."

Chapter VIII: The Dream

Gaspar took us to the building besides his observatory. It was a nice building made also of two floors but both had bedrooms with four poster beds. All of the bedrooms in that building were similar. Gaspar informed us that these were the guest rooms and we were to choose any of the rooms we liked. Meanwhile, Feroz asked permission to leave in order to go check up on his family. Liu Shang, Hao Chan and I chose adjoining rooms on the second floor. Gaspar went back into his study and asked Hao Chan to meet him there after we were done unpacking our bags.

We didn't have much in our bags and so we were done in a short time. Hao Chan excused himself and left us while Liu Shang and I decided to rest in or comfortable beds until dinner time. As soon as I laid my head on the white pillow, I drifted off into a very peaceful dream. I was in a field at night. There were five or six people that I didn't know beside me with some sheep and goats. Everyone but me was looking up towards the sky. I looked up and saw the most beautiful vision I have ever seen. Though it was late at night, the sky was alight with what seemed to be a star. But it was close to us and looked as if it was hovering just a few feet above our heads. As we looked at it, a very beautiful music started and there was some singing accompanying the music. I couldn't make out the words but the whole scene and the music were exhilarating.

I felt happy and energized when Hao Chan knocked on my door at dinner time. I quickly washed my face and went back to Gaspar's observatory for dinner. We didn't talk about many things over dinner but the discussion was more than enough to drive the dream out of my mind. I couldn't make out what it meant then.

The rest of the week before our new departure passed quickly. Hao Chan spent most of his time with Gaspar in the study while Liu Shang and I spent most of our time walking around the city streets and beaches. We only met with Hao Chan and Gaspar for short periods during meals and talked about what we had been doing and what else we planned to do later. Also, Liu Shang started teaching me a bit of the Roman language since it was the language I would need from now on. He told me that he'd teach me as much as he could of it during our trip.

Finally, the week was over, our wagon was packed and we were ready to make our way to Lansura to meet up with Larvandad. Gaspar and Hao Chan discussed their last details and we were off towards the west. This journey wasn't expected to take more than a month, but due to some weather complications, we were set back by a couple of weeks. Eventually, we got to Lansura and Larvandad had sent someone to meet us at the city gates.

Chapter IX: The Star

Our escort led us through the city streets straight to Larvandad's castle. I had seen some castles in my life and this one wasn't much different. We were told to wait in the guest hall where Larvandad would meet us soon.

A few minutes later, a man who appeared to be in his sixties with a long white beard opened the door and joined us in the hall. Gaspar recognized him as Larvandad and hurried to greet him.

"Welcome my friend," said Larvandad, "I am glad you made it safely."

"We encountered some snowy weather on our way here," replied Gaspar, "but we eventually made it."

"And I see you brought guests too," exclaimed Larvandad looking towards me and Liu Shang expectedly, "pray introduce them!"

"Definitely," answered Gaspar happily turning towards us, "This is Liu Shang, a former disciple of mine and this is Vishnu, a seeker of spiritual knowledge."

"Glad to meet you fine people," said Larvandad smiling, "I believe that Gaspar knew that you'd benefit from my discovery and thus brought you with him."

"Indeed my friend," answered Gaspar, "they are both bright minds and able souls. I hope I have not offended you by taking this initiative."

"Never Gaspar," scolded Larvandad, "on the contrary, you've done well in bringing these fine men here. You know that it is our duty to share whatever we come up with."

"But, in your letter, you sounded as if the knowledge you have was dangerous and shouldn't be shared."

"I fear that it might be misunderstood. That's why I need to discuss it with you first."

"And what is the origin of your knowledge?"

"As usual, the stars."

"Excellent then. Shall we head to the observatory?"

"Why the hurry Gaspar? Take it easy my friend. We have plenty of time and I bet you and your comrades are hungry."

"Now that you mention it, we are hungry."

"That's settled then, follow me to the dining hall."

Larvandad showed us the way to the dining hall where a delicious looking meal was already waiting for us. We ate and drank until we were satisfied and couldn't eat anything else anymore. Then, Larvandad wanted to get more acquainted with Liu Shang and me.

"So tell me about yourself Vishnu," he said, "what have you learned so far?"

"I don't know where to start," I replied hesitantly, "I heard a lot about the Luciferic, Ahrimanic and Angelic forces. Liu Shang explained these to me while Gaspar explained more about astrology and divination methods and how to use them in order to find out what I should do on my journey. And we also talked a bit about Karma."

"Interesting," he exclaimed, "you talked about Karma? What did you learn about it?"

"Gaspar set some of my ideas about it straight," I explained, "he told me that it's located in the spirit and that when all Karma is done, the world will find true peace."

"That's true. Only then will God's kingdom set itself here on earth. However, the problem with our world today is that there is a very little number of people working on finishing Karma, which is making the whole process rather slow. We have to learn to work with Karma together."

"But Karma is individual and each person has his own Karma. We cannot help with other people's Karma!"

"Yes we can, but only a very small number of people know how to do it. These people are the enlightened souls who, through conscious effort, where able to overcome mental death and chose to come back as human beings in order to relieve the world's Karma."

"Like whom?"

"In India, we have the Avatars such as Rama and Krishna. In other regions we have other people who were able to spiritually help a huge number of people. Zarathustra, Moses and many others were among these few. The problem is that they don't come often. They only come when the world is way out of balance."

"You mean that they only come when the Ahrimanic and Luciferic forces are very powerful?"

"The world and people are like a pendulum swinging between Luciferic and Ahrimanic forces. Initially, the pendulum is stable in the middle: that's when Angelic forces are strongest. However, when it is shaken even a little bit, both Ahrimanic and Luciferic forces start to exercise a pull on the pendulum consecutively. Eventually, balance is restored. However, when the pendulum rocks way out of control and there is a risk of complete annihilation because both Ahrimanic and Luciferic forces are out of control, the need for external intervention rises and so, the Angelic forces call upon divine intervention which shows up in the form of one of the Avatars like those I mentioned earlier."

"Why don't the Angelic forces always call upon divine intervention? It would make things much easier."

"You think that Ahrimanic and Luciferic forces are evil, don't you?" replied Larvandad with a gentle laugh, "Well, they are not. They are as necessary as the Angelic forces. In the world, we need order as much as we need chaos, otherwise the world will arrive at a standstill and no progress is then possible. If you forcefully held the pendulum at stasis, it wouldn't be a pendulum anymore, would it?"

"I guess not. But what does that have to do with the world?"

"The world needs order and chaos to function; otherwise, it would be dead. Look at a river. The water in it is moving from the source to the sea systematically. Also, when we look at the water more closely, we see that it's gushing and splashing here and there chaotically surging with life within it. If we remove order and chaos from the river, thus reducing it to a pond, it becomes a source of disease and distress, even though there is still some order and some chaos in it."

"I see. Without the conflict between order and chaos, there is no life."

"Exactly. Divine intervention is only called upon when things get way out of hand. In their nature, people always tend slightly towards one force or the other. However, an effective human being who can really accomplish something worthy on the level of Karma is the person who can keep the forces balanced within himself. He must always be aware of the forces within him and never let them get out of hand."

"And that's when helping with the Karma of others is possible?"

"In a way, yes. We, as people and not Avatars, have a big role to play in helping end the world's Karma. I haven't understood how this can be done yet; however, I believe that my discovery will lead us towards the answer."

"Tell us then about your discovery, Larvandad," interjected Gaspar.

"I believe we have talked too much today. Let us meet at my observatory tomorrow at nightfall and we'll talk about it," replied Larvandad.

"You sure know how to tease a man Larvandad!" joked Gaspar.

"You have waited more than a month to learn it," answered Larvandad smirking, "a day will not kill you Gaspar."

Larvandad sure kept us awake that night. We were all very excited to learn what Larvandad had in store for us. I forced myself to fall asleep because I wanted time to pass as fast as possible. We were so relieved when morning came, but that was only half the time until our meeting with Larvandad. Just to make the time go by faster, we decided to walk around the city streets and maybe do some fun things. That day seemed longer than the whole month that we spent travelling. But finally, night fell and, guided by Gaspar, we found our way to Larvandad's observatory.

The observatory was much bigger than Gaspar's observatory, but it was very similar in many ways, and especially the window in the ceiling. However, Larvandad had different sized windows located in different parts of the room. There were also more than one window in the ceiling and all of them were open. Larvandad was standing beneath one of them and looking up through it. We approached him slowly. He looked towards us and called Gaspar to his side.

"Look at this Gaspar," he instructed him.

"What is this?" asked Gaspar surprised.

"It has been getting clearer and clearer ever since I saw it a few months ago. And it's moving."

"Moving? How?"

"Well, since I have been observing it for a few months, I could see where it used to be and where it is now and I tell you, it is moving."

"That's interesting. I've never seen anything like this before!"

"Me neither. I tell you it shocked me a lot when I started to notice its movement."

"But what does it mean?" asked Gaspar ponderingly.

"I don't know, but the only thing that I truly feel is that I should follow it and see where it's headed."

"You mean that this could be a sign for us?"

"Definitely. I haven't noticed any worthy signs recently and then this star or comet or whatever shows up."

"You're right. But in which direction is it headed?"

"It's headed southwards, possibly towards Egypt."

"Then that's where we should go!"

"I'm glad you share my passion old friend. Let's go together then."

"I'll go too," added Liu Shang.

"And so will I," I exclaimed finally.

"That's terrific," cried Larvandad, "the four of us shall go on this quest."

"When do you want to leave?" asked Gaspar.

"In a week or two at most," answered Larvandad, "I need to notify the court as well as my deputies of my absence and tell them what should be done. Then, I will be ready to leave."

"Great," replied Gaspar, "this would also give me the chance to monitor the movement of the star myself too."

"That's settled then," said Larvandad, "I suggest you enjoy what the city offers until I'm ready."

"I think I should go send a letter to Hao Chan and inform him that my absence would be longer than expected," added Gaspar.

"Yes," replied Liu Shang, "send him my sincerest regards as well."

Chapter X: Hao Chan's Problems

We headed back to our rooms in the guest wing within Larvandad's castle. A few minutes later, Gaspar called us so we went to his room.

"Hao Chan sent a letter," he exclaimed as he opened the piece of parchment. We closed by him and read it:

Dear Friends,

Feroz and I are fine; however, things here in Jenikand aren't too well. In the beginning, I was able to maintain an appropriate level of trust with the people. A few weeks later, this trust started wavering and especially because they claimed that I am not one of them, which is reinforced by my Chinese looks. I am in desperate need of help and I hope that you can come back soon.

Sincerely,

"What are we to do?" asked Liu Shang.

"I have to go back!" said Gaspar, "but I can't. I have to go with Larvandad. Otherwise, I would've come all the way here for nothing."

"Isn't there another solution?" I asked, "Maybe to try and remind them that you are the one who appointed him in your stead."

"We could try sending a letter with my seal on it," answered Gaspar, "but it will not do any good if Hao Chan's Angelic forces are weakened."

"Then one of us should go help him," concluded Liu Shang, "but who?"

"Vishnu is our best chance," explained Gaspar, "the way back to Jenikand is easy; however, the way to Egypt is as yet unknown. We as rulers have more diplomatic connections and need to stick together in order to get there. We cannot break our bond."

"Fine then," I sighed, "I will go back to him. But how will I be able to follow you to Egypt afterwards?"

"After you get to Jenikand and restore order," answered Gaspar, "ask for Ashanemah. He is a merchant and knows the best way to Egypt. After you get to Egypt, locate the star we are following and head towards it. If all goes well, we will meet underneath it."

"One more thing," I added, "I don't know how to make my way back to Jenikand alone."

"Yes, of course," replied Gaspar, "I will ask Larvandad to spare one of his men for you to guide you there."

"And when should I leave here?" I asked.

"Tomorrow noon," answered Gaspar, "I'll need some time to inform Larvandad of the problem so that he could lend us one of his men."

I wasn't too happy about the prospect of going back now that we were so close to our objective. However, I was the only one capable of doing this mission. The others had to stick together. I didn't sleep that night but started packing my bags and arranging my room. Gaspar went back to Larvandad's castle during the night to inform him of our problem. When the early rays of the morning sun started shining into my room, there was a knock on my door. I opened it and saw a man waiting for me. He informed me that he was Aydin and he'd be my companion back to Jenikiand. Aydin was almost twice my size and muscular. He seemed to be the best man for the job. He helped me carry my bags into a new, smaller carriage that Larvandad provided for our journey back. After we finished packing, Gaspar handed me the letter with his seal on it, we bid farewell to everyone and were on our way.

The weather was a lot better than the one we encountered on our way to Lansura. Aydin was a very good companion despite his frightening attire. However, he wasn't into the spiritual world at all. As I understood from him, he was one of Larvandad's soldiers who had enough geographic knowledge to get me back to Jenikand quickly and in one peace. And he was successful. Due to the small size of our carriage and his sharp memory of shortcuts, our journey didn't take more than three weeks.

Finally, we arrived to Jenikand. Everything seemed to be peaceful, though there was a strange tension in the air. There were people in the market doing their shopping, merchants filled the streets and children played near the houses. But still, things didn't feel well. I could somehow sense that the people were afraid. Aydin informed me that he would be resting for a few days and then leaving back to Lansura. I made my way to Gaspar's home where Hao Chan was now residing. I knocked on the door and Hao Chan himself opened it. He looked at me for a couple of seconds before he embraced me tight and let me in, closing the door behind us. Feroz was inside too but he was sitting behind the office busily scribbling on some parchment. He barely looked up and greeted me before getting back to work. I told him about Gaspar's delay due to the journey to Egypt.

"I thought Gaspar would come," started Hao Chan, "but I'm glad they sent you."

"How come?" I asked.

"I've been depressed for some time now," he answered, "things here are becoming worse every day."

"Why?"

"I'm not one of them. I'm Chinese. I look very different from them and so, they don't trust me readily."

"But things were going fine for the first few weeks, haven't they?"

"Yes. That time, I always stayed here and didn't go out. So the people didn't know me. Feroz did most of the talking for me. However, one day, I needed to go out and help sort out a mess between two villagers who were at a dispute regarding some property."

"Then what?"

"Then, after I gave my opinion on the matter and told them what must be done, the man who was wrong started calling me names related to my Chinese origin. I didn't answer him of course, but Feroz heard many more villagers calling me the same names too after that incident."

"So?"

"I'm afraid that there might be a rebellion soon. The people might overthrow me and then Gaspar would come back to find his kingdom in ruins, just like Yutian."

"Don't worry."

"How can I not worry? If Gaspar came, he would've solved the matter quickly. However, they sent me you. Not that I have any complaints, but you are a foreigner as well. What can you do to help?"

"I have a letter signed from Gaspar."

"It's of no use."

Hao Chan was becoming very negative and tough to persuade. I tried talking some sense into him, but he wouldn't listen. He was convinced that he failed although there was no rebellion yet. Then I remembered something he did to Liu Shang when the latter was starting to give up hope.

"Hao Chan listen to me," I shouted. He calmed down and listened, "Don't let the Luciferic forces take over you!"

"Huh?" said Hao Chan with a blank look on his face, "what?"

"You are letting the Luciferic forces take over you. You are making a mess out of nothing. Calm down for a bit."

Hao Chan took a deep breath and closed his eyes. Then, he opened them again, turned around and went to another room. I tried to follow him but he asked me to wait where I was for a bit. He needed to be alone for a moment. So I stayed with Feroz.

"What did you do to him?" asked Feroz suddenly, "I was listening to everything you said but I don't understand how talking could do that much to a person."

"It's like a password we use among ourselves," I explained, "when one of us is upset and cannot control himself, we remind him of the Luciferic and Ahrimanic powers. This makes him think about it and so control his anger or fear."

"I don't want to know," sighed Feroz with a confused look on his face, "Gaspar's meaningless babble never made sense to me anyway."

I started laughing. Feroz smiled and then bent back upon his desk and continued his work. A few minutes later, Hao Chan emerged back out from his room with a smile on his face. He seemed to be a whole new person now. The Hao Chan I knew was back.

"Come with me," he said as he went out the front door, "bring the letter with you."

"Where are you going?" I asked.

"Feroz," he called, "follow us."

We followed Hao Chan through the city streets towards the town center. It was a large court with a bell in its middle. Hao Chan headed straight to the bell and started ringing it. Slowly, the people of the city gathered around us. Then, Hao Chan started talking in a very loud voice so that everyone could hear him.

"People of Jenikand," he called.

"What do you want, you Chinese bastard?" cried back one of the townspeople.

"I have just received a letter from King Gaspar," continued Hao Chan as if the man hasn't spoken at all, "the king is on a quest and will be absent for more than four months probably. He is currently on his way to Egypt. Meanwhile, he appointed me, as you already know, as ruler in his place. I know that I am not one of you. I know that most of you hate me for this. But regardless, I promise you that I will do my utmost best to rule Jenikand as honestly and as justly as possible. I do not want to cause problems. I want peace and prosperity to this land. King Gaspar appointed me in his stead and I will not disappoint him. That is all I have to say to you."

There was an awkward silence for a couple of minutes. Everyone including me was shocked at Hao Chan's new found courage. Then, he muttered under his breath just loud enough for me to hear him "May the Lord's will be done." Suddenly, Feroz shouted from behind us: "Hail King Hao Chan! Hail King Hao Chan!" The people, as if they were waiting for someone to start, echoed Feroz' cry happily. Hao Chan smiled and greeted the people.

Chapter XI: Back on my Way

The tense atmosphere started to loosen from then on; the people became more collaborative with Hao Chan and slowly began to actually like him. In a few weeks, everything was peaceful and prosperous again because Hao Chan was happy and positive. Now, it was time for me to head to Egypt. Feroz helped me locate Ashanemah. He was a merchant who travels between Jenikand, Mesopotamia and Egypt transporting, buying and selling artifacts.

Ashanemah was in his forties. He had graying hair and was slender. He wore a white turban on his head and drove a carriage similar to the one Aydin brought me here in. Ashanemah was happy at the prospect of having someone travel with him to Egypt, but he insisted that I pay. It wasn't such a problem but he insisted on taking all the gold that my father gave me. Desperately, I gave him the money and went with him. I did keep a few coins for myself but didn't let him know about them. I put my bags in the back along with his merchandise and we set off.

He wasn't a very nice man; however, he informed me that we will be making a stop in Baghdadu. He said that most of his customers were there and he had some merchandise that they ordered. I could do nothing but agree with him. I had to get to Egypt one way or another because the others were waiting there for me.

Our journey started early the next morning. It was as boring as it was uneventful. We traveled by day and slept in the tent during the night because Ashanemah was stingy enough not to want to pay for an inn, and especially for two people. Gladly, the weather was hot and we didn't have to encounter any rain.

Finally, the first half of the journey was finished and we were in the busy city of Baghdadu. We arrived there around noon and I've never seen a city more crowded than this one. Suddenly, I had a bad feeling about things. I somehow knew that something bad was going to happen soon. In order to try and be ready for it, I decided to observe what was going on. Women with baskets on their heads were busily doing their day's shopping, merchants had set up their tents and were calling on their merchandise and others were moving on in carriages through the city streets. As we went on our way, I noticed a temple somewhere. I suddenly had the urge to go inside. I informed Ashanemah of my intentions and he proposed to join me.

He tied his carriage to one of the poles beside the temple and we got off. Suddenly, I got another feeling of fright which was even stronger than the one I felt before. Then, as this feeling kept growing and growing, we felt someone creeping behind us fast and put their swords around our necks.

"You'd better not move," said the voice of the man who was behind me. He seemed to be wearing something around his face because his voice was somehow muffled.

"Yea," said the other, "we're going to take your carriage and go away with it gently. If you move, we will kill you."

Ashanemah didn't heed their call and struggled to get out of the bandit's grab, but the bandit was too strong for him and didn't hesitate to cut his throat. Ashanemah wasn't even able to shout for help as he fell to the ground in a puddle of his own blood.

At the sight of this terrifying murder, I couldn't hold myself anymore and I shouted at the top of my lungs. As I did, I felt a strong blow to the back of my head and I fell to the ground.

Chapter XII: The Dancer

I woke up again feeling dizzy and with a terrible headache not knowing what had happened. It took me a while to focus again and try to determine where I was. I was in a well lit and huge room. I could see a dome above my head. When I moved my head which was still aching, I saw that there were many pillars around this room. There were also many statues of different sizes and shapes. From the look of things, I knew that I was inside some sort of temple in the middle of which was an altar.

There, besides the altar, was a woman in a yellow dress. She was very beautiful, more than anything that I have ever seen. She was dancing with her eyes closed. I couldn't take my eyes off of her. The dance she was performing was as beautiful as she was.

She moved so gracefully as if she and the wind were one.

Then, she opened her eyes, looked at me and smiled. She gracefully walked towards me and sat beside me.

"Hello," she greeted me, "I hope you feel fine."

"I have a terrible headache," I replied trying to sit up straight, "Am I in the temple?"

"Yes you are."

"What happened to me? I don't remember anything."

"It seems that you were attacked and robbed."

My memory started to sharpen and I remembered the thieves and the swords. Then, in shock, I remembered Ashanemah.

"What happened to Ashanemah?" I asked.

She looked to the ground and didn't say anything. I knew that he hadn't survived.

"Where is he now?" I asked.

"We cremated him," she said, "we didn't know how long you were going to be unconscious and couldn't leave him there."

"I see. How long was I out?"

"Two days. You took a heavy blow on the back of your head."

"Who brought me here?"

"I did. When I saw you outside the temple, I couldn't leave you there and so, I brought you here."

"Thank you. I don't know how I will be able to thank you for I have nothing now."

"Don't worry about it. All this is in the service of the Lord."

"May He bless you."

"He already has. You're new here, aren't you?"

"Yes, I am," I replied.

"Where do you come from?" she asked tenderly.

"Jenikand," I answered, "but I initially come from India."

"I miss India," she said in Indian.

"You're from India too?"

"Yes I am. My parents and I moved here when I was six years old and I grew up in this city."

"I see. By the way, I liked your dance very much!"

"Thank you. It's my way of communing with the Lord."

"That's interesting. I personally prefer meditation."

"To each his own way of worship. Some people like to meditate, others prefer bowing, and some just kneel and pray while others, like me, dance or sing."

"And does it work?"

"What do you mean?"

"Does dancing help you commune with the Lord?"

"Couldn't you see it?"

"See what?"

"The force surrounding me."

"The what?"

"Let me start from the beginning then. You seem ready to learn."

"How can you tell?"

"I can see it."

"Well then, go ahead."

"I assume you know about Ahrimanic, Luciferic, and Angelic forces."

"Yes," I said hesitantly. I wasn't aware that so many people knew about this.

"Well, with proper training, you will be able to see them and recognize them."

"So far, I only thought that they were invisible."

"They are. But with the proper tool open, you will be able to see, or actually feel them. Sometimes, you feel bad when you are with a person. Other times, you feel that you and a person will be friends for life. Where do these feelings come from?"

"The heart?"

"Yes. Exactly. Your heart is the organ which tells you what kind of energy is in a person. If you have similar energies, you like that person. If you have opposing energies, you don't like this person."

"But this only works with Ahrimanic and Luciferic forces because Angelic forces are different in nature."

"In a way, you are right. However, you can consider that Luciferic and Ahrimanic forces are both the opposites of Angelic forces."

"I see."

"So if you have Luciferic forces in you, you will feel comfortable with people who have them, but you will feel awkward or a sense of dislike towards people who have Ahrimanic forces within them. If you have Angelic forces in you, you will have a bad feeling when you are around people who have either Ahrimanic or Luciferic forces within them but you will automatically be friendly to people who are working with Angelic forces."

"That makes sense. Would people with Ahrimanic and Luciferic forces feel anything towards people with Angelic forces?"

"They would definitely be irritated, but if played well, people with Angelic forces can quiet down the others and awaken the Angelic forces within them."

"But how can you sense this force?"

"Everyone can sense it, but only faintly. You can develop it by letting go of yourself."

"I know. I sensed it around Ashanemah. But how am I to let go of myself?"

"When you communicate with any person, intend to merge yourself with him. This is done when you choose to love that person even if you don't know him. When you can love any person you see, you will know what forces play within him."

"I don't understand."

"When you choose to love someone, that love will take one of three courses. The first course is returned love. It's when that person loves you back unconditionally. This happens when two people with Angelic forces meet. The second course is when an Angelic force meets a Luciferic force. The Luciferic forces are chaotic in nature and therefore, this love would be similar. It would be a very chaotic love which doesn't last long and neither lover would understand it. It would be more like an addiction to the other than it is a love. As for the third course, when an Angelic and an Ahrimanic force love, the tendency for the Ahrimanic force to maintain order will be displayed through that person's need to have the relationship under control."

"But the forces in a person are constantly changing."

"Exactly. That's why people change and their love changes as well."

"In this, you are talking about romantic relationships. But what about normal friendships?"

"Friendship is also a love, although devoid of sexual attraction and romance. Before you marry your wife, you have love for her. Love is there but it's devoid of sexual and romantic intentions. This love could remain a love as it is or it could acquire sexual and romantic attraction and become what we call marriage."

"But I would love my wife more than I'd love my friend, wouldn't I?"

"There are no degrees in love. You cannot love something more than something else. You either love it or you don't. You may prefer it to another thing, but that doesn't mean that you love it less. Sexual desire and romantic attraction aren't related to love. They are added to it simply because we view love not as giving, but as getting. When we love someone, we love him for our benefit, not for his. And because of this, love changes. When you want to marry, you perform an elaborate act or dance to attract your lover. If you ask me, this is similar to animals in many ways. The male or female would perform a dance so that they attract their significant other in order to breed. They want the other to relieve their own desires, not to give to that person and work on making him happy. Animals don't need to fall in love to procreate, neither do some people."

"That's true. But now that you said it this way, it seems so wrong."

"I know. That's why we have to change our perception of love and awaken to its true reality. We have to love for the other, not for ourselves. We have to shift from looking for getting love to looking for giving love. Only people with Angelic forces can do that because they are at ease."

"What you are saying is in accordance with all the ancient teachings. We have to love others like we would love ourselves. But only now do I see it and understand it right. I've always understood love as unique and exclusive to one person. Now I see how the Avatars could love everyone, even their enemies."

"They just gave and gave regardless of who was receiving their love. Like the sun, it shines upon the good and the evil, the black and the white, the man and the woman. It gives regardless of who receives and yet, when sunlight strikes anything, its colors appear clearer.

Sunlight brings out the color in things. Love is like that, when someone receives love, he will appear healthier and better looking. This is because of the happiness that love brings. The sun is the source of light; the Lord is the source of love. When we accept His love, we will let it shine through us. However, when we decide to hide from it in the dark and refuse to let it into us, we become dark and dull. That's what evil and hatred are."

"Beautiful!"

"Very beautiful indeed. And it's our job to share this love with everyone, and especially those who are afraid of it and hide from it. If we can let our love shine upon them, we will be able to reveal their true colors and help them love in their own turn. That's why love cannot be limited to one person. When you have the Angelic forces working within you, you have the Lord's love flowing into you regularly and quickly. You cannot keep this love to yourself. You have to share it. And you can't share it with only one person because it's bigger than both of you. You have to share it with everyone."

"I feel like I want to hug everyone now."

She laughed.

"Why are you laughing?"

"You have just experienced what a dose of love is," she said while she approached to give me one of the best hugs I've ever felt, "Throughout all my conversation with you, I was sending you love. I sent you so much that it filled you and now you feel that it's too much that you want to give away. That's what real love feels like."

"But how did you do it? Can you teach me?"

"When you talk to someone from your heart and when you tell them everything you know with a passion, you send them love. However, when you lie to them, you bring them down and you steal love from them. Whatever you say or do, let it be with love. Remember, it is love which gives meaning to marriage and not marriage which gives meaning to love."

Talking to this woman made me feel so warm on the inside. I felt as if I had known her all my life. The way she talked with me was truly angelic. I hadn't realized it, but as time flew by, it seems that we left the temple and were now in what probably was her house. All the time, her angelic energy was filling me to the brim until I couldn't take it anymore. My feelings of love swelled up inside me until I could no longer master them and then, without thinking, I did it. I kissed her right there and then. I could feel her smile as she kissed me back and embraced me. We stayed locked in a frenzy of emotions inside the temple. Time flew by so quickly that, before I knew it, night had fallen. Her love carried me into a different world. All my problems vanished without a trace, as if they weren't there to start with. I completely forgot where I was until I opened my eyes and looked around.

"Oh no!" I exclaimed as I realized what I had done.

"What is it?" she asked sweetly.

"I shouldn't have done this!"

"Why not?"

"We should be married!"

She laughed her usual sweet laugh.

"This is not a laughing matter."

"What is marriage?"

"Marriage is when you become my wife in front of the Lord."

"Where is the Lord?"

"He's everywhere, of course."

"Then He already knows we're married?"

"But we have to get legally married in a temple!"

"So we should get married in front of a religious person, not the Lord?"

I laughed myself when I realized my stupidity. We didn't really need all that legal stuff to get married. The fact that we loved each other so deeply is enough proof for ourselves that we are married. We're faithful for each other and have no problem spending all our lives together if we could. But…oh no. We couldn't. I have to continue my journey. I can't stay here. Suddenly, I looked at her as she smiled, which made me lose track of my thoughts.

"What is your name?" I asked her, "I just realized that I don't know your name."

"Anuragini, what is yours?"

"Vishnu."

"Nice name."

"So is yours."

Slowly, I came out of my world with her and started remembering my problems in the outer world. I realized that I had no one to continue my journey with and that I'm alone in a place where I don't know anyone. She suggested that I spend the night with her in her home.

Her home was small and she lived alone in it since her parents had passed away some time ago. She cooked a very delicious Indian dinner which brought back all the memories from my home and my parents. I realized how much I had missed them since it was more than a year that I had been far from them.

There was only one bed in Anuragini's home and she didn't hesitate to share it with me. In her arms, I fell into a very deep and peaceful sleep.

Chapter XIII: Stuck in Baghdadu

I woke up the next morning to the sound of a rooster. A few minutes later, I started making out the sounds of the busy streets outside town. I sat there in bed wondering what I am to do next. I couldn't continue my way to Egypt and I had no way of returning home since I had no money at all. Even the few coins that I had left were stolen. She woke up and sensed my confusion.

"Calm down," she exclaimed, "Why are you so tense?"

"I am lost and I don't know what I am to do now."

"You are welcome to stay with me for as long as you like."

"But what would people say about you if they see me with you?"

"Are we doing anything wrong?"

"But people will see it as wrong!"

"People have a tendency to see anything different as wrong. This is a natural Ahrimanic tendency to keeping things as they are. We mustn't let them affect us because, in the eyes of the Lord, we are one."

"Are you sure that you are comfortable with me staying here?"

"I'd love it. In the meantime, I could help you by divination. What is your form of divination?"

"What do you mean?"

"Which method of divination did you choose as your preferred? The one you resort to when you get stuck somewhere."

"I wasn't aware that I had to choose one."

"You don't have to choose one, but it's better that you do. In that way, you'll know exactly what you have to do when you get stuck."

"What is your method of divination?"

"I prefer Tarot reading and sometimes may use the I-Ching."

"Can you teach me about them?"

"Yes, but it would need some time for you to learn the details."

"It's ok."

"And another thing is that you don't have to do it exactly like I do it or in the same way that anyone else does. They are personal methods of divination and you may make your own way of using them as long as that way stays the same."

"Can you do a Tarot or I-Ching reading for me?"

"Sure. Come with me."

Anuragini and I went to the adjoining living room. She opened a cupboard and extracted a small wooden box. Out of that box, she took out a deck of cards wrapped in a sheet of purple velvet cloth. She told me that they were the Tarot cards and started arranging them in a certain way on the table. I couldn't make much sense of the pictures on the cards or of their significance, but she seemed to be getting more and more interested with every card she turns. Finally, after a few moments of doing this, she spoke.

"It seems like our fates are more interconnected than I thought," she said.

"What do you mean?" I asked.

"The cards are saying that your sign is on the way, but it will be a bit late."

"So?"

"So, I suggest that you stay still and wait for it with me."

"I guess that I don't have any other choice anyway."

"Exactly."

She smiled and put the deck back in the cupboard and closed it. She then went to the kitchen and prepared a breakfast for the two of us. I stayed in the living room thinking and wondering alone.

"Still worried?" she asked me when she came back with the breakfast.

"Now what do I do?" I asked exasperated, "how will I get to Egypt now?"

"Why do you need to get to Egypt?" she asked me.

"My friends. They are meeting me there. I have to find them."

"But why in Egypt?"

"We were following a star and I had to go to Jenikand to fix some matters then meet them there."

"Remember what the tarot said. Stay put and wait for the sign. It will come when it should."

There was nothing else for me to do. So I stayed with Anuragini. My days with her transformed to weeks and weeks transformed to months until we discovered that she got pregnant. We weren't officially married or anything and we didn't care. We knew that our love was beyond marriage. However, the coming baby worried us because we wouldn't be able to provide. The money she had from her parents was almost finished. I could've written for my parents and asked them for money but this seemed to be a very bad idea, although I stayed in touch with them and they were more than happy to learn of me and Anuragini. So, I needed to find a job.

I didn't want to work in anything related to buying and selling, even though it was a very common job here in Baghdadu. I was lucky enough though to find a job at an inn. I was one of the waiters and served food to customers. It wasn't such a big job and the pay wasn't that good, but it was enough to support my new family, and the days passed quickly between work and home.

A few months later, Anuragini had a baby girl and we called her Aashi because she brought a smile to our faces. She became the center of our lives and we vowed to give her all the love and the wisdom we had. And the years passed by.

I kept my regular job and my patron was a very good man. He would always ask me to bring my daughter along to work because he wasn't married and had no children himself. So, I brought her with me regularly and he would always have some presents ready for her. He treated her as if she were his own.

All this work and this new life made me stop thinking about the reason of my being here in Baghdadu. I had forgotten even the faces of my old comrades until the day one of them came into the inn.

Chapter XIV: Hao Chan's Return

I was cleaning one of the tables after some guests had left; someone came in and went to talk with my patron. A few minutes later, my patron called me so that I'd show that new arrival to a table. It was Hao Chan. At first, he didn't recognize me because of my graying hair, but after taking a good look, he embraced me so hard I thought I would choke.

"Finally," he cried as tears crept into his eyes, "I found you."

"I'm sorry old friend!" I replied, "The circumstances overcame me and I had to stay here."

"I looked all over for you," he said, "Then I went to India and your parents told me that you'd be here and I came after you."

"But, my parents never said anything about you having asked about me."

"They probably didn't recognize me."

"Tell me, how are they?"

"They are fine. Still spending the gold they got."

"Good to hear that. What about Liu Shang and the others? What happened with them?"

"They didn't go to Egypt after all. The star stopped somewhere in the Near East where they met the new Avatar."

"What? A new Avatar?"

"Yes. That's all they told me. They couldn't explain more than that. It seems like they were somehow tongue-tied. I heard from one of their escorts than they were forced to visit the Roman emperor there. They seemed to not have liked that meeting much which caused them to get back to their kingdoms in a hurry."

"They all went back to their homes?"

"Yea. Larvandad went back to Lansura. Gaspar and Liu Shang are at Jenikand."

"And why did you come after me?"

"I was worried about you so much. When Ashanemah didn't come back, I knew that there was something wrong. Then I thought that your first impulse might be to go back to India but I was mistaken."

"I had to stay here."

"But why?"

"You see the girl playing with my patron?"

"She's your daughter?" guessed Hao Chan with a look of surprise creeping up to his face, "Congratulations and many blessings."

"Thank you," I replied proudly.

"So much has been happening with you. I thought you'd maybe want to come with me to Egypt now."

"Egypt? Why?"

"Well, the star stayed a bit over the Near East and then it continued moving towards Egypt. I'm not going to spend my life without seeing the avatar. I believe he is in Egypt now."

"I wish I could go with you. But I cannot leave my family behind."

"That's a pity."

"Listen, why don't you join me back home after I finish my work for today? I want you to meet Anuragini, my wife."

"Sure my friend."

Hao Chan rented a room in the inn where I worked because I didn't have enough place back at home to receive him. After I finished my work, we met at the guest room and then he came with me to my home. I introduced him to Anuragini and he had dinner with us.

"You're lucky to have her," said Hao Chan.

"And I am lucky to have Vishnu," replied Anuragini before I could swallow my food to answer.

"So," he said, "will you change your mind and join me on my road to Egypt?"

"No," I answered, "I need to stay here and work to provide for my family."

"Why not move to Jenikand?" he asked, "Gaspar and Liu Shang would be more than glad to provide and care for your family while you finish what you have to do."

"What is he talking about?" asked Anuragini, "I think you should go."

"What?" I asked in surprise, "but I can't leave you."

"Father," spoke Aashi suddenly, "I want to go to Jenikand."

"But you don't know where Jenikand is sweetheart," I replied.

"Is it quieter than here?" she asked.

"A lot quieter," I answered, "there aren't as many people there."

"Then I want to go," she said firmly, "I don't like the noise here."

"There you go," said Anuragini with a gentle smile in the end, "even Aashi says that you should go."

"But," I couldn't think of anything else to say. Everyone wanted me to go.

"That's settled then," concluded Hao Chan, "all the signs say that you should come with me. We set off in a week. That should give you enough time to set your affairs here in order."

"Yes," I answered as I remembered the Tarot reading that Anuragini had given me on our second day together, "but I need to see my family off to Jenikand safely."

"Your family will be leaving to Jenikand as soon as we leave to Egypt."

"How?"

"Gaspar knew that it might come to this when I told him where you were. So he sent another wagon with me. One of Gaspar's trusty drivers is driving it and he will take your family to Jenikand as soon as they're ready."

On the next day, I announced to my patron that I would be quitting and he refused to let me go before seeing Aashi again. Before we left, he brought her the biggest doll she has ever seen as a farewell present. He was truly sad that we were leaving because he felt that we were the family he never had. In the meantime, Anuragini arranged all our possessions. Hao Chan and the driver helped her pack them into the wagon. We unfortunately had to leave some things behind.

Chapter XV: To Egypt

This week went by quickly because we were all extremely busy. Finally, the two wagons were ready. The smaller one was mine and Hao Chan's and the bigger one was Anuragini's. We were off again chasing dreams and running after stars.

Though it had been years that I had interrupted my journey, now that I'm working on it again, I could remember everything about it vividly. All the excitement was coming back. I shared with Hao Chan the knowledge I received from Anuragini about love. He informed me that the others had learned much from their journey and Larvandad had his question answered.

"What was his question again?" I asked.

"He wanted to know how we, without being avatars, can help finish the Karma of others."

"And you say he got it answered?"

"Yes, but he refused to tell me the answer. He insisted that you and I should go find it out for ourselves."

"What about the star they were following?"

"As they traveled, they noticed that it stopped moving for a while somewhere they didn't recognize well. They refused to get into details because they were afraid that information about the Avatar might land into the wrong hands prematurely. It could be related to their meeting with the emperor."

"Then what?"

"The star stopped moving for a couple of years and then it started again. Larvandad concluded that it moved towards Egypt. Its movement is somehow slower now, but it's still moving."

The journey alongside Hao Chan was exciting and calm. Hao Chan was still the same person he used to be despite the years we spent in different worlds. We traveled for three weeks until we arrived to a town called Zeugma which is halfway between Baghdadu and our destination. We decided to spend the night at an inn there because sleeping in a tent for three weeks wasn't doing our backs any good.

I woke up the next morning feeling better than usual; however, Hao Chan wasn't feeling good at all. We found the closest doctor in the area who came and checked up on him. After going through the necessary procedures, the doctor told us that Hao Chan was suffering from high fever. He prescribed some herbs for him but, I could see it in his eyes that Hao Chan was terribly ill.

I was determined to help my friend so I asked the doctor for more details concerning the herbs and where they could be found. He gave me some of them and told me where I could find the others. I spent the rest of that day looking for the herbs. I had to ask some people to help me while I hunted for others myself. Eventually, I was able to gather them all and administered them to Hao Chan as the doctor instructed. We decided to stay at the inn until Hao Chan gets well enough to continue our journey.

On the second day, Hao Chan was still as ill as the day before. I faithfully did what the doctor had instructed me to do. They did relieve some of the pain and helped Hao Chan go to sleep, but they didn't help in getting rid of the fever. It was the same over the next few days. All this time, Hao Chan was rarely able to keep any food in his stomach because he would vomit anything that he ate.

Two weeks later, Hao Chan's health was still bad and started getting worse. He looked paler than before; he lost much weight and was eating less every day. In addition to that, I was running out of herbs and needed to get him some more. So I went back to the doctor who even prescribed some stronger herbs which I got. From my discussion with the doctor, I could understand that Hao Chan was hopeless. I returned to the inn brokenhearted, but I pretended as if all was going well so that Hao Chan wouldn't worry about me. As I made him some tea that night with the herbs the doctor gave me, he gathered some of his strength and started talking to me.

"I am going to die soon," he started, "I can feel it coming at last!"

"Don't say that," I replied, "you will be fine."

"I know myself well enough to know that I will not survive this," he said with a smile.

I didn't know what to answer to that. I remained silent.

"Anyway," he continued, "promise me that you will go see the avatar with or without me."

"But this was our journey. We are supposed to get there together."

"Don't worry; I will be with you wherever you go. Remember me when you meet the avatar."

"I will do that. But please, try and get better because I don't want to go there alone."

"You are never alone. My spirit will be with you even if my body is not. I need you to promise me something else, too."

"Sure, what is it?"

"Don't grieve for me when I die."

"I cannot promise you this. You are my dearest friend and ..."

"You are my dearest friend too. Think of my death as a separation. Imagine you being here while I'm in another part of the world."

"But if that were the case, I'd be able to visit you when I need you even if it has to take me years. If you die, I will never be able to see you again."

"Yes you will. I am inside your mind. When you remember me, I come back to life in your mind. After all, memory and imagination are one and the same."

"No. In memory, you remember what happened with you and the people you know. On the other hand, in imagination, you create things and events which never happened."

"Can you remember anything exactly as it happened?"

"No. I forget some details."

"And sometimes, you may fill these gaps with false memories."

"Maybe."

"Memory, my friend, is an imagination of an event that has really happened. That's how they are one. And so, when you remember me, I pray that you do it happily. Don't remember me with grief in your heart, enjoy all the happy memories we cherished together," he paused for a minute and coughed, "Why do we live here?"

"To be happy."

"Then, only remember what makes you happy. It will do you no good to remember me in this state, whereas I will live on in you and your children if you keep what I taught you alive in your heart. That is the best way for keeping me alive."

"Save your breath my friend. You've talked too much and you should rest."

"One more thing though."

"Yes?"

"Remind Liu Shang of what I told you now when you see him."

"I will. Don't worry about it."

With this, Hao Chan took his tea and started sipping it slowly. I could see from his eyes how bitter it tasted and I felt as if he was only drinking tea so as not to upset me. I slept by his bedside that night because he wasn't feeling good at all. The tea made him relaxed enough to be able to sleep. On the next morning, he didn't wake up.

Chapter XVI: A New Companion

I had never broken a promise in my life until that day. I couldn't help keeping my tears to myself. Hao Chan was a friend anyone would be honored to have. I tried as much as I could to calm myself down. After many attempts at remembering what we discussed last night, I was able to ease up a bit.

The rest of the day, I didn't remember what I did. The doctor and the innkeeper helped me a lot in cleaning up. I didn't know what Hao Chan would've liked us to do with his body and I didn't know anything about his traditions so I decided to honor him according to mine. In the afternoon, we set him on a pillar of wood and set it on fire.

After all was finished, I couldn't bear staying another night in the inn although the keeper insisted that I stay free of charge. I didn't want to be sad anymore because Hao Chan wouldn't have liked it. I moved my stuff into the carriage and went on my way, still following the star.

That night, I didn't sleep and I didn't want to. I kept going and going. The whole day went by with me rather absent minded. I didn't know where I was nor where I was going and I didn't care. Finally, the next night, I was too tired to go on.

I needed to get some sleep, but I didn't know if there were any villages in my vicinity. I tried to look around me to see if there were any lights coming from nearby towns, but there was nothing giving light except the moon and its fellow stars. Also, I didn't have the energy or the willingness to set up a tent for me to sleep so I made some room for me in the back of the carriage.

As I slowly drifted into a deep sleep, I started dreaming. It was a familiar dream that I had seen before. The star floated above the head of me and some shepherds. Beautiful music filled the air. Then I woke up. It seems that a ray of sunlight which passed through the carriage's covers woke me up. This was in addition to the sound of sheep and cattle beside me. I climbed out of my covers and went outside. It was around midday. As my eyes were trying to adjust to the light, one of the shepherds approached me.

"Greetings," he started, "I'm sorry for waking you up."

"Not at all," I replied, "I should be thanking you actually. I have to get on my way now."

"Where are you heading?" he asked inquisitively.

"Egypt," I answered.

"Where in Egypt?"

"I don't know."

"Egypt is a huge land. You could even get lost easily on the way."

"I won't get lost."

"Have you been there before?"

"No."

"Then how will you know that you are on the right track?"

"I just know. Why are you asking?"

"Last night, there was a bright light coming from this part of the clearing. I didn't dare approach it at night so I decided to come see if I could determine its source by day. And that's when I found you."

"Interesting. I didn't notice anything at all last night."

I was surprised. Especially that in my dream there were both shepherds and a strange light. I didn't want to look too shocked in front of him because I didn't feel too well around him and his sheep. Despite that, the relation between my dream and what that man was telling me seemed to point towards something. Could this be a sign? I didn't know but I decided to continue my discussion with him to see if he had something important to tell me.

"That's weird," he continued, "the light was so bright you couldn't miss it."

"Maybe it was because I was too tired that I didn't see it."

"You sure look pretty tired. Why are you going to Egypt?"

I didn't know if it was safe to trust him with the information I had. I didn't know if he would understand me or if he would think that I'm out of my mind. Then, I reasoned that, if the dream was a sign, then I should trust that man with the information I have. And I did. I told him my whole story from the beginning till now. He listened intently. Finally, when I was done telling him my story, he was quiet and silent for a while.

"If what you are telling me about the star and the avatar is correct - and I assume it is - then I have been a very insensitive father," he said regretfully as he sat down on a rock under a tree.

"Why?" I asked as I felt that my dislike for the man started to disperse. His Angelic forces were probably starting to take over.

"My son," he recounted, "he studied a bit of astrology with a sage who died a few years ago."

"Yes?"

"I always thought that all this astrology business was nonsense. He saw that moving star and wanted to follow it but I forbade him."

"I see."

"He is back at home now, busily studying his charts. I hope you could come and meet him. You seem to be a very knowledgeable man."

"Why not?"

The man gathered his sheep and we went to his house. I went in my carriage because I didn't want to leave it there for bandits or stray animals. It took us a couple of hours to get to his home. It was a little cottage at the foot of a mountain with a small stable behind it. He locked away the sheep and released my horses with his horse which was already there so that they'd rest for some time. Then, I went inside with him. His wife, a somewhat short woman in her fifties, greeted us and he introduced me to her. She was very cordial and nice to me. She started preparing some dinner while the man and I went to his son's room.

He knocked the door and we entered. The room was in a state of chaos. Books and papers littered the floor, the tables, his bed and everything else. The son, a slender man with black hair who seemed in his twenties, was busily scribbling on a piece of paper on a table in the corner of the room with his back to us. He didn't turn around to see who came in. We made our way through the heaps of books and his father called to him.

"Efram, I have someone to see you," announced the father.

"Tell her to go away," answered Efram without lifting his head, "I'm busy."

"He thinks that the neighbor's girl is here to see him," murmured his father to me, "she loves him but he doesn't even look at her."

"Efram," I said.

"Who are you?" he asked and turned around, "What do you want?"

"Why are you so rude?" asked his father, "I asked him to come see you because he was telling me about the moving star you saw."

"Oh!" said Efram surprised. At that moment, the Luciferic forces in him seemed to begin to disperse, "are you following it?"

"Yes, I am."

"I wanted to follow it too but he wouldn't let me," he looked back at his father and rolled his eyes.

"It seems to have slowed down somewhere over Egypt. That's not very far from here."

"But," interrupted the father, "you still need to find a ferry there."

"A ferry?" I asked, "I was thinking of going there by land."

They both looked at me in shock and then burst into laughter. I didn't understand why they were laughing.

"Are you out of your mind?" asked Efram, "you want to cross the desert of Sinai?"

"There's a desert up ahead?" I asked.

"Yes, there is," answered his father, "and you'd be out of your mind to cross it alone and with your horses."

"True," added Efram looking excited, "you'd need someone to come along with you."

"You want to come along?" I asked.

"Only if he'll let me," he said looking at his father expectantly, "he thinks astrology is nonsense."

"Even if it were nonsense," replied his father, "now I feel better about you going since you have someone to accompany you."

"So," I said, "you want to trust me - a total stranger - with your son's life?"

"You're not the only one who believes in signs," answered his father, "the light I saw where you were is a sign that I can trust you."

"Fine then," I replied, "When do you want to leave?"

"At the soonest possible," answered Efram, "I've waited too long."

"It's going to get dark soon so you'd better spend the night here and be on your way tomorrow morning," said his father.

"Very well then," I replied, "but from where will we be taking a ferry?"

"The nearest port is in Sur," replied Efram, "it's one of the best in the area."

"How much time will we need to get there?" I asked.

"Between one and two weeks," he answered.

Efram's mother entered the room and called us for dinner. Her cooking was delicious and reminded me of Anuragini's cooking. I remembered how much I missed her and my daughter. After dinner, Efram rushed to his room. I didn't know what to do so I followed him soon afterwards. I knocked and entered to see him busily piling up the books and papers and arranging them on shelves and on the table. I came in to help him on one hand and to check out the books he has on the other. He had quite a huge collection of books and documents on astrology that he must've spent a whole fortune for.

"How did you manage to collect these books?" I asked him.

"Most of them aren't mine," he smiled, "they used to be my teacher's. He told me to take them after he dies because his children would most likely throw them away."

"I see," I replied, "why are you so interested in astrology?"

"The night sky fascinates me," he answered wide eyed, "I can't seem to take my eyes off of it."

"Then you must've seen the light your father saw yesterday."

"Unfortunately, no. I was too busy trying to see if the star had moved."

"And?"

"It seems to have stopped again. But I cannot be sure because I need more time to determine that."

"What do you think you'll find if you follow it?"

"Something great I expect. Do you know what's underneath it?"

"From what I've heard, the new avatar is underneath it. He also has the answer to an important question."

"What's an avatar?"

"An avatar is an incarnation of the Lord on earth to help the people and to save them."

"That sounds a lot like what we call the messiah. According to traditions, he's supposed to come and save us."

"Names change, but he's the same."

"Anyway, do you really think we'll find him?"

"Yes, I hope so."

"I'm getting excited now! What do you think he'll do?"

"He will teach us how to help one another finishing Karma and making earth a peaceful place."

"What is karma?" asked Efram.

"We will discuss it on our way," I replied, "what matters is that we're working on it now."

"I hope so."

Efram seemed to be very nice and I was glad that he would be travelling alongside me. God knows I needed a companion. I was also glad that I gave Efram's father a chance to talk; otherwise, I would've met my fate in the desert alone. I started to feel much better and much more at ease now. Efram and I finished arranging the room and I brought my sleeping covers from the carriage because he insisted that I sleep in his room so that we could talk more. He was eager to learn from my experience and wanted to discuss what he knows to evaluate his own spiritual progress. All in all, he was a very wise person but, because he spent most of his time in the room among books, he wasn't so used to being around people anymore. Efram was like an overgrown ten year old with the knowledge of an old man. The way he asked questions and awaited answers was very childish. He made sure that we discussed Karma fully during the night and even took some notes. No wonder his father wouldn't let him go on the journey alone. He somehow reminded me of myself when I was his age.

Chapter XVII: Iskandariya

On the next day, as I expected, Efram was up long before me. I suspect that he even waited for me to fall asleep before he left the room and started preparing for his journey. When I woke up, my carriage was ready, breakfast was ready, Efram was wide awake and double checking if everything was in order. We sat together with his parents for breakfast. He was eating so fast I prayed he wouldn't choke. I hurried with my food too because I know how hard it is to wait for someone. That's how it began with me and Hao Chan. He was so patient that he made an extra effort to make me wait longer.

After we were done with breakfast, Efram moved the rest of our belongings to the carriage, including my sleeping covers. Meanwhile, his father called me aside to talk to me.

"Listen," he said, "you probably noticed how Efram behaves, haven't you?"

"Yes," I replied.

"I need you to promise me that you will take good care of him. He is my only son. With your experience, I know that you can turn him to a strong man."

"Don't worry about that. I will keep him safe."

"Thank you."

I went to the carriage where Efram was already waiting and we were off. I could feel Efram's energy rising higher and higher with every turn of the wheels. Somehow, I knew how his journey was going to be.

Despite the fact that Efram was rarely leaving the house, his knowledge of the roads was very good. He knew where every road leads and where every inn was. He also knew all the shortcuts, which made our journey much easier. It took us eight days to reach the docks.

Sur was a very busy city probably because of its port. The noise of the buyers and the sellers in the market merged with that of the sea and of the ships coming in and out carrying people and merchandise from all over the Mediterranean. Efram was wide eyed and his head kept moving in all directions trying to take in all that was going on around us. We asked some people who came in our way if they knew which ships would be going to Egypt. We got many answers so we went aboard to talk to the captains. We spent the whole day going over from ship to ship until we eventually chose the one we would be boarding. We took our belongings aboard and I sold the carriage and the horses for the first price I got, which wasn't much, but I didn't care. We had enough money to buy at least four carriages when we arrive in Egypt. We were informed that we would be docking again at the port of Iskandariya in two weeks.

We set sail and were on our way. These were the longest two weeks of our lives because we had nothing to do. We were just passengers on a ship. Our fellow passengers were mostly made of merchants. We spent most of our days just staring at the sea and talking. Efram started to open up and behave less childishly. It was probably because he was trying to imitate my own behavior. I hope I can be a role model for my daughter as I am to him.

The two weeks were up and we docked in Iskandariya. The weather was hot, unlike the weather in Sur. It was in the late afternoon when we disembarked the ship so we had to find a place to spend the night. Fortunately, there were many inns available. We stayed in one of them. We were so tired from our travels that we didn't even have time to discuss anything before we fell deeply asleep.

On the next day, the first thing on my agenda was to buy a new carriage to transport ourselves and our baggage. I found one similar to the one I had for a reasonable price so I bought it and we moved our bags into it. By the time we were done, night was starting to fall so we started looking for the star. It didn't take much for us to locate it and we could see that it was almost above us now. We determined the direction we had to follow and were on our way. We made plenty of progress that night but had to stop as soon as daylight set in because we couldn't see the star anymore and we needed to rest. We proceeded a bit during the day and found a village close by. We rented a room there and slept until the late afternoon.

As soon as the sun set, we had a light dinner and set out to continue our journey. It was almost the same as yesterday, but the weather was somewhat cold and when we arrived to the next village on the next day, Efram was starting to feel sick. I suggested we stay at the inn for two days but he was intent on continuing. As we proceeded our journey on the day after, he started getting worse and worse but he was still bearing and intent on continuing especially as we were now almost right under the star. That night, despite the cold weather, we felt warmer and warmer as we approached the area below the star until finally, we found ourselves in a village. It was quiet because most of the people were asleep. This village was right under the star. We left our carriage tied outside and went in. We walked around the city streets until we were besides a house which felt different and warmer. We knew that the avatar was there. We couldn't just knock and enter at night, so we stayed in our carriage and waited until it was daylight and the people were awake.

That night, as we sat in the carriage waiting for daylight and thinking about the following day, Efram started coughing and feeling sicker. As soon as the sun was up and the village was back to life, I took him to the nearest inn and found a doctor for him. According to the doctor, Efram was suffering from a mild fever which should disperse in three or four days at the most and was supposed to stay in bed for most of that time so as not to make it worse. Efram looked downcast because he wanted to see the avatar so much he couldn't wait.

But I insisted that he waits because the avatar wasn't going anywhere and if he were, we would know. That day, I wanted to stay with him but he insisted that I shouldn't wait and I should go and see the avatar first so that I have something to talk to him about while he got better. I found this reasonable and so I waited for him to fall asleep and then I went.

Chapter XVIII: The Avatar's Answer

The village was surging with life. The market was filled with sounds and noises of people buying, selling and bartering. Women had jugs of water upon their heads and were heading home. Horses with chariots passed by from time to time adding on to the noise of the busy streets. Children were busily playing games near one of the houses.

I walked through the village trying to take in all that surrounded me. As I passed by the playful children, one of them caught my attention. He was about four years old with slightly tanned skin. He sat alone on the stairs leading up to the house I saw last night. I looked up to the house and saw a woman standing by the window. She was busily working on something I could not see. What a woman! As I stared at her, she seemed to grow even more beautiful. The smile never left her lips as she busily worked and occasionally glanced towards the child on the stairs. Her hair was partially covered with a veil but her beauty was breathtaking.

Then, I moved my sight back to the child and was amazed by his radiant beauty. I've never seen anything like this before. The sight of it warmed me up and I couldn't but stare. This child was definitely not of this earth. In all the people I've met on my journey, I've never seen something as beautiful and as magical as him. I just stood there and contemplated this beauty for as long as I could remember. I couldn't move my eyes away from him.

Suddenly, as if to acknowledge my presence, the child - if that's what he was - looked up towards me and smiled. Then, he gestured me with his hand to come closer. My heart was filled with joy. I hurried on and bowed near him. Being this close to him made the warmth and the radiance coming from him even more distinct and powerful. I lost myself besides this being. I couldn't think nor move anymore. There was nothing I wanted more than being right here, right now. This is what I had been looking for. This is the truth I needed.

The child put his hand on my shoulder. I lifted my head and looked up. My gaze met his eyes and he stared deeply into me. Now, I completely lost myself and felt that I had become one with him, no, one with everything. In his eyes I could see everything. I became everything. I felt true peace. Love was everywhere. He filled everything and everything was in him. What a miracle!

In his divine gaze, everything made sense. All my questions were answered and then seemed trivial. My entire journey came to its end but I could see it again from the beginning.

Suddenly, while I was still lost in that child's divine gaze, I was transported out of this earth and even out of my body. Everything around me was white. I looked around me and some figures started to appear. They were people. I looked closer and was amazed to recognize them. I could see Lord Krishna, Lord Rama, the Buddha and many others I didn't recognize but I could feel that they were equally divine people. Instinctively, I tried to get closer to Lord Krishna, but another figure appeared in front of me and blocked my way. I looked directly at it until it became clearer to me and I was extremely happy to see that it was Hao Chan. He looked extremely good and much happier. He smiled at me and embraced me. His embrace felt much different and much more beautiful than on earth.

"Where are we?" I asked, "Is this the afterlife?"

"This is a part of the afterlife of some people," he answered, "you'll understand this when you get to it. For now, let us call this the Hall of Answers."

"So this is where I get my questions answered," I said.

"All the answers can be found in life itself for those who observe nature in depth. This place is only open when the avatar is on earth."

"I see. But what does it do?"

"It provides the answers you are looking for. You see, an avatar's mission is to help you find the answers to your own questions by guiding you through the laws of nature."

"I don't understand."

"Well, ask a question and see!"

"Ok. How can we help others relieve their karma?"

Suddenly, everything went pitch black. Then, I found myself in a forest near a tree. In one of the branches, there was a mother bird in its nest with young birds. She threw one of them out. It started to flap its wings chaotically until finally, it was able to fly back up to the nest. However, when it got back to the nest, it was bigger and it took the place that the mother was keeping. It threw little birds one after another and they learned to fly. The more little birds it threw, the more appeared in the nest in their place. More nests appeared on the tree beside it as well.

After this vision was done, I was back in the Hall of Answers with Hao Chan in front of me.

"Do you understand now?" he asked.

"Not really," I answered, "I feel that this is the answer I need but I don't know what to make of it."

"Efram will help you figure it out," announced Hao Chan, "go talk to him about it."

As suddenly as everything appeared, everything disappeared and I was again in front of the child. He looked in my eyes as he was looking before and smiled a very kind and heartwarming smile. Then, he came closer and embraced me. I couldn't help bursting into tears. His mother opened the door of the house and stood besides us. She was smiling too. She bent down, picked him up gently, and took him back into the house.

I sat down on the stairs for as long as I could remember, lost in thought and in a deep feeling of ecstasy and bliss. Though I didn't understand my answer yet, I couldn't help feeling happy, as if nothing could ever ruin my mood.

Chapter XVIV: Understanding

As night started to fall, I remembered that I should be getting back to the inn because Efram should be getting dinner now. I made my way back and went into the room. Efram was awake and looked better. He smiled at me expectantly as I entered.

"So?" he asked, "did you see him?"

"Yes," I answered happily.

"What happened?" he asked, "you must tell me in detail."

I told him about everything I saw, from the child to Lord Krishna to Hao Chan to the vision and to what Hao Chan told me about the vision. He listened intently to everything I said.

"Can you tell me more about Karma?" he asked after I was done.

"Briefly, each person is born with Karma in the form of deeds, tasks, and missions he has to accomplish through his life. The collective Karma of all the people amounts to making earth a peaceful and happy place but, as long as some karma is still not accomplished, peace cannot be possible."

"Alright," he pushed on, "How does an avatar help with Karma?"

"The avatar takes on a human body and therefore claims some Karma upon himself. He chooses his karma to be greater than that of a normal human being. By living an exceptionally moral life, the avatar is able to undergo all the tasks and missions he has to undergo regardless of how tough or painful they might be. By doing so, the avatar gets rid of a lot of Karma. The problem is that we know that it is possible to help others with their own Karma, but we don't know how. That was the answer I went looking for."

"And the vision answers that question."

"How?"

"Simple. The mother bird teaches its child how to fly. The child, in his turn, teaches many other batches of children how to fly and then this child's children will teach their own children how to fly and so on. If we take it as Karma, a person can teach another about Karma. That person then teaches many others what he had learned. His students will then teach their own students about karma and so on."

"That's it! When so many people awaken and understand Karma, they can start working on finishing it and they would teach others how to do it themselves."

"So, our mission comes down to this: we have to teach others about finishing Karma and awaken them to the fact that they have to teach others about Karma and also ask the others to do the same. In doing so, we create something like an expanding web of people who work on finishing Karma and, with every generation, that number of people increases."

"Eventually," I continued as if we were both speaking as one person now, "everyone will be aware of Karma and we'll be working together to make the world a peaceful place."

"This reminds me of an old Chinese proverb that Hao Chan shared with me once: Give a man a fish and you feed him for a day. Teach a man to fish and you feed him for a lifetime."

"And," Efram continued excitedly, "Teach a man to teach another how to fish and you feed a whole tribe for lifetimes to come."

Efram and I were lost in deep thought for the remainder of the day. We finally understood how it works. It was so simple and the answer was right there in nature. I brought Efram his dinner and we went to bed.

On the next day, I woke up to find that Efram wasn't in bed. I was a bit worried but somehow felt that all was fine. I also instinctively knew where he was off to. As I put my clothes on preparing myself to follow him there, he entered the room gaily.

"So?" I asked him.

"I met him," he answered, "I met Emmanuel!"

Chapter XX: The Wedding Invitation

The years went by. I grew older alongside my loving wife and family. We lived together in Jenikand for a few years before we moved back to India to live closer to our families.

As soon as we arrived there, I learned that my old guru had passed away a few months back and someone had to take care of the temple in his stead. I didn't hesitate to fill in his shoes now that I was wiser. I felt that this could be the best place for me to be and to teach.

After then, life went by slowly and quickly at the same time. My parents passed away followed by my previous comrades. Gaspar sent me a letter informing me of the death of Larvandad while, a few years later, Liu Shang informed me of Gaspar's death. There was no one left to inform me of Liu Shang's death but I knew that he was bound to pass away sooner or later.

Despite my grief for my leaving friends, there were always little family joys every now and then. Due to my preoccupation with teaching faithful devotees in the temple, I wasn't able to be around for my family and especially my wife. We had no other children but we loved Aashi so much and taught her to be as good as anyone ever could. Later on, she got married and had a family of her own while my wife and I became grandparents.

More than twenty-five years had passed since I had seen the Avatar, but I still remember his face as if it were yesterday. I always thought about him and wondered what he was doing. I also thought about Efram who decided to stay behind and follow the Avatar. But I couldn't stay. I had to come back and care for my family.

One day, as I sat in the temple in deep meditation, a messenger entered. He had a letter for me. I opened it hastily and found out that it was from Efram.

Dear Vishnu,

It's been quite a long time that we have been apart. I was, and still am, totally immersed in following the messiah. His teachings are beautiful and he speaks straight to my heart.

Despite my preoccupation with the messiah, I still got a decent job in teaching people and explaining to them the teachings of the messiah. At first, it started out as I just explained what he says to the people who were too far and couldn't hear him well. As I kept doing this, more and more people gathered around me and some of them even paid me for my services. At first, I got upset that they paid me and I wanted to refuse this money. But, as I was returning it, the messiah passed behind me and put his hand on my shoulder. I understood that I was supposed to be grateful for people's generosity and not refuse it. The more payment I accepted, the more people paid for me and I never asked for any money nor needed to ask.

But that's not the purpose of my letter anyway. The reason behind my writing to you is that I would like to invite you for my wedding. I met the most amazing woman I could ever find. She is also one of the messiah's followers. I hope that you and your family can join us. My wedding celebration will be in the middle of the summer. I think you will have around four months to get here after you receive my letter and that would be enough time for you. The wedding will be in my house in the area of Kana.

My wife and I would be more than glad to receive you and we already have a place for you and your family to stay.

Sincerest Regards,

Your Friend,

Efram

Chapter XXI: Back to the Near East

I was so happy for my friend Efram and found no reason for me not to attend his wedding. Anuragini was also excited at the prospect and wanted to see that region for so long. I couldn't leave the temple unattended during my absence so my daughter and her husband volunteered to take care of things until I would return.

Anuragini and I were in our sixties and weren't as energetic as we used to be. We hired one of the townspeople to take us to Efram's house in Kana. He didn't know the way there but I knew the language so we could ask around until we found it. We had enough time anyway. A week later, we were on our way. Being back in a wagon brought back into my heart the rush of my years of adventure looking for the avatar. I felt rejuvenated and excited.

Most of our journey was uneventful. We passed by many of the roads and the regions that I went through before. On our way, we passed by Baghdadu and insisted on staying at the inn where I used to work. Of course, my patron had surely passed away, but the new innkeeper was as nice and cordial as my patron used to be. He even spoke in the same manner, which made me curious.

"I used to work here almost thirty years ago," I said, "what happened to the man who used to run this place?"

"My father passed away five years ago," he answered sadly.

"Your father?"

"Adoptive father actually," he answered, "My mother came here when she was pregnant and had nowhere to go. So he took her in and took care of her until she gave birth. Unfortunately, she died afterwards. She didn't say anything about who my father was or anything about my family. Also, no one in this city could recognize her. Consequently, there was no one to take me in so the innkeeper here didn't hesitate to take over and became my father. He loved me more than anything in his life and never abandoned his duties towards me. He sent me to school and then taught me how to run the place here. Then, he passed away."

"I'm glad you came around for him," I replied, "the poor fellow had no children of his own and desperately loved children. I remember how he used to play around all day with my daughter."

"Aashi?"

"He told you about her?"

"Oh yes. He told me a lot about her and about you. You must be Vishnu then, I assume."

"Yes I am. And what's your name?"

"My father loved you and your family so much that he decided to name me after you."

"I feel honored. I really don't know what to say."

"Believe me. I'm so glad to meet you. You remind me a lot of my father. What are you doing here anyway?"

"We are headed to Kana for a friend's wedding."

"Very nice. You are welcome to stay in my humble inn for as long as you please."

"We cannot stay long. We will just be resting here for a couple of days before we continue our way."

We stayed at the inn for two days and then packed up and were on our way again. Vishnu, the innkeeper, refused to let us pay for our stay and said that he enjoyed our stay very much because we reminded him of the father he loved so dearly. All through our stay, we were together and Anuragini and I would tell him stories about his father. He would listen intently and sometimes, tears would creep up to his eyes. That's when I would hug him and calm him down. Despite that, he always asked for more stories.

Chapter XXII: Efram's Wedding

Six weeks later, we were able to locate the city of Kana. Most of the people there knew Efram and didn't hesitate to lead us to his house. It wasn't actually a house but more of a mansion. It was very large and very beautiful. As we went through the gates, one of the servants came to greet us. We told him that we were here to see Efram and showed him the letter that I received. The servant turned around and went to call his master who appeared, running down the stairs to meet us. As soon as he saw me, he embraced me tightly.

"How are you my old friend?" he asked lovingly.

"I am very well indeed," I replied, "it's so nice to see you again."

"Come in," he said, "let me lead you to your quarters where you will unpack your bags and stay."

Efram led us to a house right beside his. He informed me that he had it done and ready specially for me because I will probably have nowhere to stay. He gave us the keys and informed us that we will be meeting again at sunset for dinner. He also wished that he could stay and help us unpack but had to attend to his wedding preparations.

Anuragini, our driver, and I had ample time to unpack and even rest for a while before sunset. Then, one of the servants knocked at our door and led our way to Efram's dining hall. Efram was already there and instructed us to sit beside him because we had a lot of catching up to do.

"How's life in India nowadays?" started Efram.

"It's great and peaceful. I'm now in charge of running the temple of my village."

"That's good. I know you love this."

"Yes of course. And what have you been doing?"

"I have also been teaching. I just listen to the messiah and explain to the people who were too far to listen."

"Yes, you told me this in your letter. But, how did you build all this?"

"I realized that, when people really listen to the words of God, they open up very wide and will want to give as much as they could. When they do, it happens that I'm the first person they think about and they give many valuable things to me. So, I built this house and many others around the area. However, this is the only one for me. The other houses I built were for the poor and the needy."

"That is good. And what is the avatar actually teaching you?"

"In summary, whatever he says or does springs out from love, divine love. He is simply teaching us, through his example, that we can love others just like the Lord loves us. We are not limited beings with a limited love capacity, we can love infinitely."

"That's very deep. And what about your future wife? How did you meet her?"

"She was one of the people who were listening to my explanation. We both knew that we were not meant to keep following the messiah alone and we wanted to have a family, just like you, so we decided to get married."

"I'm so happy for you my friend. I bet you will have an excellent wedding."

"I know we will, especially that the messiah is coming."

This got me even more excited about the wedding. I was going to meet the messiah again, and so was Anuragini. The wedding was in less than a week's time and Efram was more than glad to include me in the preparations. He asked for my opinion in almost everything. Over dinner, we would always open spiritual discussions and discuss the messiah's teachings in relation to our journey.

When the wedding day was upon us, the house was full of people. Everyone was happy and excited. After the wedding ceremony was completed, the wine jugs were opened and everyone started drinking. It was really good wine. However, the messiah hadn't showed up yet and I was getting worried that he would not be here.

It was late evening when people started saying that he arrived. I tried looking around to find him but couldn't really know which one he is. However, as I looked around, I noticed a person that I've seen before. It was the avatar's mother. She looked almost the same but a bit older. When I saw her, I moved my sight to the young man who was beside here and immediately felt his aura of love. His eyes still held that depth I saw when I met him the first time. I decided to go and introduce myself. When I approached him, he looked at me and smiled. He greeted me before I could speak a word and, as we spoke, it seemed as if the whole party around us went quiet.

"Hello Vishnu," he greeted me lovingly.

"You know my name?" I asked in surprise.

"We met around thirty years ago," he smiled, "and we meet again now for a reason."

"What do you mean?"

"I have something to ask of you."

"Pray continue."

"My brief stay here will be over soon, however, my mission will be far from over. I am here only to sow seeds. Later, the seeds will turn into many crops. But the problem is that the bigger the crops, the worse the corruption."

"What do you mean?"

"I'm here to teach people how to love. Love is a force that is uncontrollable and yet good. It is an infinite capacity present in all human beings but they always tend to seek to limit it whether by making laws about it or by limiting it to just one person. The infinite love that I'm sowing here will become too much that people will want to limit it again."

"You mean that the Ahrimanic forces will take over?"

"Yes, and they will be extremely powerful. My teachings will become the foundation of whole institutions which will deform them to preserve their existence. Much of what I teach will be lost and twisted time and time again."

"What can I do?"

"Preserve the story. Write it down because it will help in setting things straight once things go out of hand."

"But I don't know your story."

"Not my story, yours. Each person has an important story to tell. Your journey to find me and the things that you have learned should be preserved until it's their time to be revealed."

"I'll work on it. But won't other avatars come?"

"You are approaching a different age now. You don't need any more avatars. You will become the avatars that you seek. The truth is in you. Believe in yourselves and in your journey. When you learn to follow the flow, nothing can stand in your way and, if anything does stand in your way, it will be part of your path."

"I see."

"Remember, whatever you do, do it with love. You can do it. Go, learn and teach for only when you share the truth you learn will you learn more truths to share. It will never end but will always become more interesting."

As he said this, our voices drowned again in the sea of the noises coming from the celebrations around us. As my eyes were still transfixed on the messiah, his mother approached him and whispered something in his ear. He nodded, looked at me and gestured me to follow him. I did and we went into the storage rooms. As we went in, the servants appeared tense and worried. One of them came to the messiah and told him that they were out of wine and the wedding is still in its beginning. The messiah smiled and asked them to fill the jugs with water. They were too desperate that they did it without asking any questions.

As they filled the jugs with water, the messiah put his hands on a jug and closed his eyes. I just stood there and stared at him. On the outside, nothing appeared strange, but, there was a distinct feeling of energy in the air. The feeling kept getting stronger and stronger until the messiah opened his eyes and smiled. He put his hands into the jug and took out a sip. The water which was there had turned into blood-red wine.

I hasted to taste it and it was divinely delicious unlike anything I've ever tasted before. The servants were all shocked and relieved. It was a miracle. It was the first miracle of the messiah. Soon after the wine was tasted and everyone was ecstatic with the taste of heaven, news of the miracle spread like wildfire and soon enough, everyone was talking about it.

After they realized the miracle, they went looking for the messiah but his mother and he had disappeared and no one could find them. The party continued but it was now filled with a sense of awe and amazement. The wine jugs were totally drained by the people. Most drank as much as they could while some got bottles and filled them with the miraculous wine.

The wedding celebrations were over and all the invitees left. Anuragini and I retreated to our house for the remainder of the night still amazed at the events.

The next day, I woke up in the afternoon. As I sat in bed trying to piece up the events in my head, I wondered about what I should write. I couldn't come up with anything at the moment and thought I'd wait until the whole story was good in my mind.

We stayed for a few days after the wedding and then decided to go back to India. Before we went, I asked Efram to keep me updated on everything that happens with the messiah. He was more than glad to do so.

Epilogue

We went back to India and I resumed my duties there. The teaching in the temple went as smooth as ever and life was good in general. I devoted some time each day to work on writing the story. Although I had some of the details missing or even changed, I believe that I was able to get most of the important events and ideas into this biography. Efram kept his word and sent me a letter every now and then with all the news related to the messiah. He performed so many miracles after the one at the wedding and continued his teaching regularly. He showed us that the power of love was truly unlimited. However, his greatest miracle was when he overcame the final human obstacle: death.

And with this, I finish my story and place it in your hands to meditate and think about it.

The Angels in Training Program

Introduction

After having finished reading the story, you've probably noticed how things get connected together in a synchronistic flow. Throughout the following pages, you will be introduced to a course called the "Angels in Training" program. This program is completely free except for some minor fees which can be avoided easily if you are proactive enough.

There are two ways for you to follow the program: the individual way and the official way. The individual way can be done simply by reading these courses whereas, the official way makes you an official mentor of the program and you will be expected to teach other official participants. So far, the program can be reached though the following link: http://angels.seekersofwisdom.org

I hope to see you all there soon...

The Program

We were all born angels; however, life's experiences may alter our perception of life itself and make us lose our angelhood and maybe fall from grace. This has contributed to a general loss in happiness in the majority of people around the world.

The Angels in Training program seeks to remind those who embrace it of their angelhood through different ideologies and techniques. However, all readers should know that, by angels, we do not mean sprouting wings and flying doing all sorts of good deeds. By angels, we mean people who are happy and who work on teaching others how to spread happiness on and on.

Upon starting the program, all participants will be assigned to a mentor who will supervise and advise them regarding what is happening and what should be done. The program can be completed in 14 weeks after which the participants will receive updates of new ideas and techniques. The program is as follows:

1- Introduction to the program and getting assigned to a mentor: Participants are assigned to their mentor and get to know him/her and the program.

2- Acquiring and charging Urim: The stone of positivity

3- Charging Urim and learning about synchronicities: Getting into the flow of energy and learning the value of coincidences

4- Getting Thummim and learning to use Urim and Thummim: Learning to make choices based on randomness

5- Researching divination methods and choosing a favorite: Understanding how the universe works and how to work with it

6- Going deeper in a chosen divination method: Working on a personal divination method

7- Learning about Karma: A deeper look at the truth behind Karma

8- Learning about energy: Going deeper in matters of energy, life and love

9- Learning about the Ahrimanic and Luciferic forces: A different way of seeing and analyzing the world

10- Studying the Angelic forces: Balancing the Ahrimanic and Luciferic forces

11- Looking into the path of life and the states of living: Studying spiritual evolution

12- Learning about after death states and reincarnation: Not a necessary belief but a necessary understanding of the concept in general

13- Writing personal biography: To improve the relation between the participant and the mentor and to make the participant reflect on his path in life so far

14- Reaching angelhood and starting teaching: Learning more techniques and their uses to show the way to others.

General Rules:

- Participants must be older than 14 and must be willing to take on the full 14 weeks of the program
- Failure to follow up will lead to an expulsion of the program. A second application can be negotiated with the mentors
- Participants should be willing to become mentors when they finish their training
- Mentors have the right to refuse a participant assigned to them but, if they refuse 3 candidates in a row, they must accept the fourth
- Any mentor-participant problems must be reported to the program leader and will be dealt accordingly

Week 1

Welcome to the "Angels in Training" program. Throughout the 14 courses, you will be exploring yourself and the world around you from many different perspectives so that you find yourself and your place in it.

You should know that, if you are not up to it, you can still withdraw now and come back whenever you feel like it. However, after a week of having been assigned to your guru, leaving would mean that you would have to discuss it with the group leader when you choose to come back.

With that said, you should now e-mail the group leader and ask to be assigned to your guru. Your guru will not be teaching you because all your courses will be available in this book and on the internet link provided above (http://angels.seekersofwisdom.org). They will be labeled from week 1 to week 14. You may read what is written in weeks which are more advanced than yours, but it is advised that you do not do so in order to keep up the enthusiasm and the advancement. And that's why your mentor is here. Unless he/she tells you to move on in the program, you will not move on even if you read what is coming later.

Your mentor is there to evaluate your progress and see how effective you are becoming. He/she will also be there for you if you face any problems or difficulties even in your ordinary life. Your mentor's advice is valuable but you may choose to disregard it although at the risk of your own development.

In case you suspect that your mentor is holding you back, it is advised that you discuss it with him/her, save the conversations and then, if the problem wasn't resolved, to discuss it with the group leader. The group leader will deal with the situation accordingly.

You must note that, upon finishing your 14 weeks of training, you will not be required to teach straight afterwards but you will be put on standby and your mentor will be there for you. Later on, when your mentor deems you worthy of becoming a mentor, your status will be updated and you will be assigned a participant when available.

I will be expecting your e-mails to info@seekersofwisdom.com soon and hope that you will become the awakened angels of tomorrow.

Week 2

I assume that you have been assigned to your guru by now. If not, hurry up and do it.

This week, our main focus will be on the value of positivity. Most of you probably have seen the movie "The Secret" by Rhonda Byrne. If not, I suggest you do although keep in mind that it is just a tool for transformation and not a means for itself. If you just want to try the secret just for trying it, you will be disappointed. Make sure you have a purpose.

Being positive has many values and benefits. One of the most important benefits is that it helps you maintain an adequate level of happiness and joy in your life, which will allow you to go on with life smoothly. Being negative or positive will not change your destiny, but the quality of your life. In short, if you want a happy life, be positive.

Changing from what you are now to a positive person is not an easy task, except with the right tool, namely, your Urim. The names Urim, and later on Thummim, were borrowed from ancient Jewish tradition. In the words of the secret, for now, Urim can be likened to the gratitude rock. Urim is a white stone that you can pick up from just anywhere. It has to be white and small enough to be carried in your pocket. You must have it in your pocket wherever you go. Each time you put your hand in your pocket, you have to try and remember something that makes you happy and positive. You could be thankful for your health, you can remember your good friends, or you can think about absolutely anything which brings a smile to your face. Do this for about a week and your Urim, which, in a way, feeds on your happiness, charges up and becomes stronger. Your happiness charges Urim up and then,

Urim will be able to energize you when you feel low just by holding it.

Next week, we will discuss this more in depth and learn why we need to be positive in order to become real angels on earth.

Week 3

Since you're reading this, you must have begun charging your Urim well. By now, your Urim probably feels like a part of you that you carry everywhere. Also, you must have started feeling somewhat happier and more positive. For this week, you have to continue working on your Urim and your positivity. Meanwhile, there's something you have to think about as you charge your Urim.

Each one of us is born with a specific mission to do on earth. We will be discussing this mission in later weeks, but for now, we should accept the fact that our life, as well as the life of others, has meaning. But how do we know that we are on the right track?

There are two phenomena which answer this question. The first is happiness. The happier you are, the more you are on the right track.

The Second phenomenon, which is much more important, is synchronicity. This term was coined by Carl Gustav Jung and then explained in detail in "The Celestine Prophecy" by James Redfield. A synchronicity can be mistaken for a coincidence all the time, except when you are open minded and expect it every day. If you decide to disregard it as a mere coincidence, that's what it will be. But, if you decide to act upon the coincidence, you will see that it will start a cascade of synchronicities which end up making you really happy.

Despite the fact that synchs (short for synchronicity) should make you happy, sometimes, a synchronicity may end up making you feel bad or in a bad situation. You must keep an open mind and a positive attitude because it's not over yet. If you give up and keep feeling bad, you'll fall out of the flow, but, if you decide to see it in a positive way and as a chance for evolution, soon enough, the fog will clear out and you will see your way again.

Good luck to all of you and your mentors will be able to answer all your questions regarding that phenomenon.

Week 4

We live in a world of ordered chaos and organized randomness. In life, we have to make choices every moment. Whatever we do is based on a choice. However, sometimes, we reach a point where making a choice is hard. What do we do then?

To answer this question, let's meet Thummim. Thummim is Urim's brother. While Urim is white, Thummim is black and means the opposite of Urim. Be careful, this doesn't mean that Thummim is evil, never. Together, Urim and Thummim will help you gather energy. So, your next assignment is to get your Thummim. Just like Urim, Thummim is a stone which should be able to fit into your pocket beside Urim. When you have both of them, you have just obtained your first and most important divination tool which will help you follow the flow.

As we said, the world we live in is a world based on randomness. Quantum physics has shown us that intention has an effect of the fabric of time and space and somehow guides the universe in a certain direction. Quantum physics also showed us that intentions affect randomness. So, if we want to know where the general universal intelligence is leading us, we should look at the randomness pattern. How do we look at the randomness pattern? Urim and Thummim are the tools for that.

To use Urim and Thummim, simply assign an arbitrary sign for each, for example "yes" for Urim and "no" for Thummim. Then, put your hand in your pocket. The first one you touch is the answer to your request. I do not recommend picking more than one time because it will lead to confusion. Simply follow the first answer you get.

However, there is something to be careful about. Sometimes, you may pick one of the stones and follow its suggestion but may end up in a bad situation. Don't fret, be positive, and follow the flow till the end because, what may seem bad now, may be very good in the long run.

For this week, continue charging your Urim and go find your Thummim.

Week 5

Assuming you have been following the instructions carefully for the last month, you should now be a more positive person who knows how to feel and follow the flow. Your Urim and Thummim should have also become your trusted advisors. Now, things get a bit more complicated.

The universe isn't always about yes and no questions. Sometimes, things get a bit more complicated and Urim and Thummim would be unable to help you follow the flow. Thus, you'll need to resort to alternative means of divination. However, you must be extremely careful and not fall in the wrong ideology believing that any form of divination can tell you the future. Divination is the universe's way of showing you what is going on in the present. Your human consciousness is only capable of analyzing so much data, however, the universal mind is much grander and can analyze and interpret more data with good precision. Despite its grandness, the universal mind requires faith to access it. Basically, if you believe in the divination method you use, the method will be effective and help you in regaining the flow.

Therefore, this week, your task will be to research some of the divination methods which are available and try to find the one you feel best about.

Week 6

Last week, you've been researching divination methods. This week's message is rather short. You are expected to deepen your knowledge in just one method. The internet is a great place to learn the basics of most divination methods; however, you are the best person to devise your own method.

You don't have to abide by the rules of a certain divination method strictly, all you have to do is learn the basics and use it as you see fit. So basically, in a week's time, you should be able to know full well how to use the divination method of your choice. If not, keep focusing on it until you know it enough.

I remind you, the usage of divination is to know where you are and to provide an alternative view of the present, not the future. Word of advice; don't get too carried away by divination, limit its use to only figuring out what to do next when you're stuck or when Urim and Thummim can't provide the help you need.

Week 7

Now that you're probably feeling the flow much more accurately, we can move to something somewhat deeper: karma.

By karma, I don't mean it in any religious way. What you are going to read now is a new view of karma which is inspired by, but not taken from the religious view of karma. Religiously, karma states that what goes around comes around. From my point of view, that's not the whole truth, there's something missing.

Karma is what makes the whole word turn. It is what initiates the flow that we are talking about. It is the reason why there is a flow and why there are synchronicities. Karma is a Hindu word which translates as deed or action. We said earlier, that each person is born with a mission to do and some deeds to finish so,

in words of karma, each person is born with karma:
work to do.

Since each person is born with karma, each
person has some work to do. What happens when his
work is done? Easy enough, that person reaches
nirvana, bliss, or the heavenly state. But that's not all,
there's more. What happens when the entire world's
karma is finished is heaven on earth. And that's our
goal: to make earth heaven and to let the Lord's
kingdom come.

Now the real question is: how do we finish
karma?

The real answer is: just follow the flow.

As we said, karma creates the flow and dictates
what we have to do. Finishing it will make us happy, so
by following the flow, we should be happy, really happy
and not just temporarily happy. However, when our
happiness destroys or harms the happiness of others,

we create more karma. And that's where the theory of what goes around comes around originates from.

Now, let's put the theory of karma in the framework of the past weeks:

Synchronicity, dreams, déjà vus, and intuitions are karma's way of telling us that we are on the right track.

Being positive is knowing that whatever happens leads to the finishing of karma, even if it looks harmful on the outside.

Urim and Thummim are karma's way of showing us which way is quicker.

Divination is just like Urim and Thummim but gives us a broader perspective on what's going on. It's like seeing the events from karma's eyes.

Now that we put all that we learned in the framework of karma, things will start to make more sense. As of next week, things will be getting very interesting.

Week 8

When we go deeper and deeper into matter, things start to get simpler and simpler. What are we made of? Flesh, bones, etc... what are they made of? Cells... what are cells made of? Molecules...What are molecules made of? Atoms... what are atoms made of? Protons, neutrons and electrons... what are these made of? Even smaller particles...

The list goes on and on and on until, eventually, we find the basic component of everything: energy. Whatever exists is because of energy, which is all there is. In life, energy is found in two forms: pure energy or materialized energy.

Materialized energy is when a lot of energy is condensed in very small spaces until it becomes matter. If we see energy as air, under heavy pressure, air becomes liquid and at even higher pressures, it will eventually become solid. It's the same with energy. The more energy is confined in small spaces, the more solid it becomes. But that's not all, what we are talking about is only static energy or energy which doesn't move quickly. Energy that moves quickly cannot be confined in small spaces and thus, doesn't become solid. But before we go further into that matter, we should probably discuss the other form of energy: pure energy.

Pure energy is energy which doesn't have material form such as heat, radiation, magnetism and other such forms. This energy is ever present and may sometimes be the property of another form of materialized energy. In addition to this, materialized energy may sometimes create pure energy. Let's take a magnet for example. It is a form of materialized energy because it is made of particles. But also, it has an aura of pure energy around it, which is magnetism.

Although materialized energy may create pure energy, the latter may sometimes affect the state of materialized energy. Let's take water for example. If we heat it, thus give it energy, its particles will start to move faster and faster until they eventually disappear into vapor and stop being confined in small spaces. The opposite is also applicable. If we extract pure energy from a certain object, it will become more solid. Also in the example of water, when we cool it, it becomes ice: the solid state of water.

Now these were simple examples which aren't really about energy but about a personification of energy. However, they help illustrate the behavior of energy in human beings. Just like the elements, human beings are also subject to fluxes of energy. Simply, energy can be detected in human beings via two states: happiness and sorrow.

When we are happy, we feel as if we're flying. It's as if we are expanding. In words of energy, happiness means having energy. Now, when we feel extremely happy, which means something close to nirvana or bliss or the heavenly state, our energy has risen very high and we have expanded all over the universe, no longer confined in the small space of the body.

On the other hand, when we feel sad or depressed, we feel as if we don't want to move anymore, as if we're too heavy. In words of energy, this means that we are getting depleted and out of energy. The less energy we have, the more depressed we will become.

Now the question poses itself: where do we get that energy from?

There are three sources of energy: nature, our higher self and other people.

Many people feel that they like to have a walk in nature when they are feeling sad. That's because plants and trees generate energy as well as oxygen. As people, we cannot feed on inorganic matter. Plants transform inorganic matter into organic matter which we can consume. Likewise, we cannot energetically feed on pure energy such as magnetism and heat (although we do use it), and so, we need it converted into consumable energy. The mere act of looking at a green plant will help regenerate quite an amount of energy. Caring for plants is also a great way to energize ourselves, especially when done with love.

Another way which is used to gain energy is by tapping into the higher self through meditation or other forms of yoga, dance and sports. Rudolf Steiner's Eurhythmy is a great way of refilling ourselves with energy. Not everyone can do that (according to my opinion) because not everyone has the patience to really reach the deep states of meditation and ritual dance.

The last way through which people refill their energy is through other people. When we communicate with others or participate in any group or couple activities, a lot of energy is being exchanged. There are two ways through which this exchange happens: stealing and receiving.

The majority of people today have grown used to stealing energy unconsciously. This stealing is when we take energy from other people by playing on their emotions, especially when we're upset. When someone is upset, and therefore low on energy, that person will have a tendency to take energy from any person in the vicinity. It can be done by upsetting the other person, by telling our sad story to make the other person sad, intimidating the other person to weaken him or just playing on his nerves. All of these ways will make us feel a bit better at the expense of the other person. They are not recommended and should be monitored because we tend to do them unconsciously.

The other way of exchanging energy which is one of the best possible ways is by giving energy and receiving in return. When we intend to make people happy, and thus give them energy, we rarely feel depleted, that's because when people feel good, they tend to give off energy without realizing it. Therefore, we are no longer in the state of "taking" energy but in the state of "receiving" energy. Therefore, by consciously willing to make people happy and thus energize them, we make ourselves happy and thus receive more energy. The energy exchanged is amplified. The more energy is exchanged the more is created to be exchanged.

If the whole human awareness everywhere can be shifted to this understanding, the face of the earth will change for good. In addition to this, when one person has a critical level of energy, that person can move on to the state of nirvana or bliss of heavenly state. What would happen if every person on earth moved into this state?

As great as this vision may seem, there's one obstacle to its realization: karma. As we have said earlier, finishing karma can help us reach the heavenly state. Simply, as long as there is karma, there is no heaven on earth. However, this doesn't mean that we should start taking energy. This still means that we should be giving energy because either way, giving energy will create more energy and thus an amplification effect. In terms of physics, a body that possesses energy is a body that can perform work. Work, in Sanskrit means karma. So, the more energy we have, the more karma we can do.

As future angels, it's your job to awaken people to this truth which is the core idea behind this whole program and remember: the terms energy and love can be interchanged.

Week 9

The world we live in is as mysterious as it is fun. As strange as it may be, with careful observation, we can start to comprehend that it is made of a balance between two polar opposites: order and chaos.

Traditionally, these two forces were called Ahrimanic for order and Luciferic for chaos. The Ahrimanic forces are named after Ahriman, the god of order while the chaotic forces are attributed to Lucifer. These two forces are in a constant struggle for power. Wherever we look, we can see them. If we look at a river, we can see that it is orderly flowing from source to sea while the water inside it is splashing around chaotically.

Both of these forces are as good as they are bad. We cannot name one good and the other evil because we cannot really see which one is better than the other. Now some of you might be thinking that order is better than chaos. That is not true for order is as good as chaos. Imagine a world with perfect order… everything is always the same, never changing. Sure it may seem good at first, but then, it turns into a boring hell. We are alive now because we have evolved, order alone cannot serve evolution for if everything was always the same, nothing would ever change and evolution would never occur. Without chaos, the world would've become a huge, lifeless machine.

On the other hand, if chaos alone existed, the world would be a real mess. Nothing would ever be the same or even similar. Adaptation would've been impossible. So, neither the Ahrimanic nor the Luciferic forces alone are beneficial, but together, they are the forces that make our world turn and evolve. The Luciferic forces break the order and provide newness while the Ahrimanic forces help the rest of the world adapt to the changing of the situation and thus, evolution occurs. However, when either of the two forces overcomes the other, catastrophes happen until balance is restored again.

In us, the Ahrimanic and Luciferic forces also exist in a balance. Our whole body works in an orderly Ahrimanic way while our mind, with its countless thoughts banging to and fro in our heads, portrays the Luciferic forces. The thoughts emerge from the head chaotically and then are ordered by the body while being executed into action. That is the archetypal operative mode of the human being. However, this is usually not the case in reality. Some people sway more towards the Ahrimanic forces while others sway more towards the Luciferic forces. Usually, the swaying is not too dangerous to pose any real threat, however, sometimes, it becomes very dangerous. An example of people with too much Ahrimanic forces within them is the person who exploits the work of many people so that he increases his hoard without really needing that much money or possessions. As for a person with too many Luciferic forces, we can find many thugs and terrorists who look only to cause chaos and mayhem.

These two cases show up when one type of forces has accumulated too much in one person. However, there is another phenomenon which we must pay attention to: forces of a similar orientation will attract similar forces. People with Ahrimanic forces will form alliances with people who have excessive Ahrimanic forces as well while people with Luciferic forces will attract people with excessive Luciferic forces. When too many people of one kind gather, signs of danger start to show up. Soon, all hell breaks loose. When one group hoards the majority of the possessions, the other group will not tolerate this and the revolution begins. The hoarding done by the first group was a sign of the accumulation of Ahrimanic forces until it reached a critical stage, and thus, the opposing forces, the Luciferic forces, had to fight back and thus, the hellish revolution.

Knowledge of these forces is extremely important for an angel in training because the angel has to keep his Ahrimanic and Luciferic tendencies under control so that the Angelic forces are allowed to perform their work. For this week, meditate well on the Ahrimanic and Luciferic forces.

Week 10

In summary of our last session, we agreed that the Ahrimanic forces are the forces of order while the Luciferic forces are the forces of chaos. We also got to the point where we said that both forces are as good as they are bad. Without them, the world as we know it can never exist and yet, an excess in one of them may be catastrophic. Today, we will talk about the third force in the triad: the Angelic forces.

As you can sense, this lesson will be the first step into angelhood. The Luciferic and Ahrimanic forces are always swaying to and fro, like a pendulum. The human soul always fluctuates between these two. If a lot of Ahrimanic forces were present, we can expect that the pendulum will soon jump into an excess of Luciferic forces. This fluctuation will continue and diminish, unless otherwise re-provoked, until balance is restored. When neither Ahrimanic nor Luciferic forces are being exerted on the human soul, there is balance and thus, the Angelic forces start to show up.

When a person is filled with Angelic forces, he/she will have a clear mind and will be able to get back on the track of karma. The stronger the angelic forces in you are, the more resistant you will be to Ahrimanic or Luciferic fluctuations. But what causes these fluctuations to happen?

The answer to that question is simple when we look at the whole picture. We strive to reach a balance between Ahrimanic and Luciferic forces so that the Angelic forces in us can emerge and start working on karma again. And, as we know, karma itself can be somewhat unsettling sometimes, especially when it's difficult. Therefore, the fluctuations in the internal Luciferic-Ahrimanic pendulum are a result of non other than karma. The divine plan is a stroke of genius! Our struggle against the Ahrimanic and Luciferic forces is a part of our karma as well. Therefore, the closer we get to finishing our karma, the less fluctuations we will have and the more stable we can become. Eventually, no more fluctuations will happen and we will always be surrounded with the Angelic forces, just like the saints and the mahatmas.

The Angelic forces make us enter into a state of giving and receiving, not taking. A person with Angelic forces will want to give as much as possible to anyone. To get to that stage, we must be aware of the three forces within us and be able to predict what's going to happen next. By doing that, the forces will be balanced much faster than if they were left at their own pace.

Week 11

Balancing the Ahrimanic and Luciferic forces in order to reach a state of Angelic forces is rather difficult, but not impossible. One key element is living in the now, escaping the past and future. What's next? What are we to do when we are living in the Angelic forces?

Just like people with Ahrimanic forces attract people with Ahrimanic forces and people with Luciferic forces attract others with Luciferic forces, people with Angelic forces will attract others with Angelic forces. That's the secret of synchronicity. When you are at peace, you are following the flow. When you are following the flow, the synchronicities which happen will be very valuable and useful. Just pay close attention to them, don't resist them and they will take you to where you should be: happiness.

One thing you should be careful of is falling back. When you are following your path, you will feel a growing confidence. Beware this confidence so that it doesn't become overconfidence. If it does, you will fall back into the pendulum of Ahrimanic and Luciferic forces.

That's it for this week. My advice to you is to take it easy. Work on balancing the forces within you and everything should be fine.

Week 12

We are all headed towards one single point towards which every single living organism is headed: death. We are all going to die some day, that's natural. However, fearing death is neither natural nor normal. Since there is no escaping death, why should we fear it? Why should we fear the unknown? Is it really unknown?

Theories abound regarding the state of death. Not one theory has been or will ever be proven correctly, however, when we look at near death experiences, we can come up with a certain conclusion: death is as stable as people's minds, which means that it's very unstable and ever changing. In Near Death Experiences (NDE), people often say that they experience almost the same things until they reach the final stage where they see a certain divine presence.

Christians say that they see Christ; Buddhists see Buddha and so forth. This means that what happens after death is related to people's beliefs here on earth. If you believe in Christ, you'll be with him, if you believe in flying pigs, you'll meet them there. Then what?

When we look at what happens in life, we see a tip of the iceberg called life of which death is a grand part. Before we look at what happens after death, let's meet the soul before it enters the body. Back then, the soul is a part of the whole and is the whole. When it takes physical form, it acquires some karma which is attributed to this form. Before birth, the soul sees its karma and develops a way to do it, knowing that it would be close to impossible to actually do all this karma in this life. And also, since the soul will be compressed into a small physical form, it will be subject to a lot of loss, most of which are memories. Effectively, when the soul gets born, it knows nothing and struggles to try and remember. That's why, the universe, God, arranges itself in a way to suit each soul's needs and experiences. It does so by crisscrossing certain people's destinies as well as some major events. That's where synchronicities are born. This is done through a struggle between the Luciferic and Ahrimanic forces as the soul is getting ready to be born. Synchronicities are signs from the universe to tell us that we are on the right track and that we should keep going this way because that's where our true experience, our true happiness, lies. Other forms of signals from the universe are dreams, intuitions and even Déjà Vus.

Then the soul takes physical form and goes through some of life's experiences...or not. When we disregard a synchronicity, we fall out of synch with the universe and are no longer following the path that we should be following. This is the birthplace of what we might call "evil". Thus, evil is not really evil, it is only the ignorance of our true path in life. When we awaken to this truth, we will be able to follow our path in life and fulfill God's will for us on earth as in heaven. Heaven? What is heaven? Do heaven and hell really exist?

After the soul's brief journey on earth, it moves on to the new dimension of death. The normal, unenlightened soul which didn't know the reality of life and death will carry on some of the mind's illusions after death. These illusions of heaven and hell are subject to each person's "conscience". If a person has a clear conscience, he will go to an illusion of heaven, no matter how he conceived it in life. If he doesn't have a clear conscience, he will go to his illusion of hell, also as he conceived it during his life. But, since both are illusions, they will diminish over time until the soul is purified of its physical remains and merges with the universe again to retake a physical form. The illusions diminish overtime because too much of one thing makes that thing meaningless. Too much happiness in heaven will make it boring because happiness without sorrow isn't happiness. As for hell, too much pain will cease to be pain overtime and will take a person to a state of indifference. Thus, both the illusions of heaven and hell become meaningless and render the soul indifferent. That's when the soul gets freed from physical desires and is ready to tackle physical life once again, this time trying to be less attached.

Contemplate on this idea for this week. We are almost towards the end of our path together and you have surely grown well.

Week 13

Now that you went deep enough into the spirituality of angels, it's time to reflect on how things have been. This is done through writing a personal biography. No, you are not expected to write a book nor remember all the details. You are only supposed to focus on your changing character and the turning points of your life.

Generally, the biography must not exceed four pages and should be written backwards. This means that you have to describe where you are now and go back in time until your earliest memory. It is usually divided into three major parts which are based on your age.

You should focus in your first part about your current situation and the major turning points in the period between the age of 14 and 21. Make sure you include how the Angels in Training program affected your life in addition to the people who had an important effect in this epoch.

In the second part, you should concentrate on describing your childhood between the age of 7 and 14. A lot of change usually occurs in this phase so you should be careful in choosing which has been a major turning point in your life.

In the third part, your main point is your early childhood between birth and the age of 7. Now you probably don't remember a lot about this, but if you reflect on it, you will see how your parents' personalities have shaped the way you behave and act. So, in this part, you should focus on your parents' and siblings' effect over you.

While writing your biography, you will start to see a very clear picture of how the events in your life were synchronistic and had all been leading you to this moment in time. You will understand how everything is leading you towards a certain purpose. After you're done writing it, you should share it with your mentor whom you should be very close to at the moment. Your mentor will discuss it with you and help you make sense of the things that are happening with you in case you didn't notice them yourself yet.

Good luck on your biography and I know that this will probably be the most dreaded yet enjoyable tasks in this program.

Week 14

After 13 weeks of reflection and rewriting your own personality, you've finally become an angel. But, the word angel actually means a messenger. You have now learned the message quite well. This week, we will just wrap up by discussing some tips and ideas regarding being an effective messenger.

First of all, you should know that whenever you encounter any problem in teaching the participants assigned to you, you can refer to your mentor who will help you solve your situation. In case your mentor can't, he/she will ask their mentor as well until a solution is reached. There are three rules you should learn when being a spiritual teacher. They are empathy, acceptance, and a sense of humor.

Empathy is when you can visualize yourself in the situation of your trainee and feel what they are feeling. Not everyone has an easy life or will change easily, that's why you should be patient and empathetic. Only when you can put yourself in another's shoes will you be able to help them overcome their tendencies and problems in order to transform them into angels. To be empathetic, you must listen with your heart, not your ears and eyes. To you, people's problem might seem insignificant, to people, their problems are the world's problems. Accept this fact and deal with it accordingly. Make a person's life and problem your own, yet remain distant. Be close to your trainee, but be yourself.

Also, in this training program, we get all kinds of people. There are only 2 things which can disqualify a participant's application. They are age, which should be more than 14, and laziness. No trainees who are less than 14 are accepted because they are not yet ready to write a comprehensive biography. Lazy people are also not accepted because the mentor is not supposed to do a person's training instead of the person himself. A mentor has plenty of participants to take care of. Participants who aren't serious will not be allowed to proceed with the program. Except for these two disqualifiers, no participant is ever refused no matter what his religion, ethnicity, race or gender is. If, as a mentor, you have an issue against any of this, you should discuss it with your mentor in order to find a solution for it. If left untreated, this is a huge problem for you.

Finally, a sense of humor is extremely important for a mentor. I have never learned anything from a teacher who was serious all the time. My favorite teachers from whom I learned most were the funniest people I've ever met. A tense atmosphere produces no learning. A simple joke, smile, or funny gesture dissipates a tense atmosphere in seconds and costs nothing at all. To be a good mentor, be witty, funny and alive. Don't be dull and boring.

In the end, my dear angels, I wish you the best of luck on your newfound journey. Know that, through this, you are helping relieve the word's karma. Before I end this last week, I'd like to share with you again one of my reshaped quotes:

"If you give a man a fish, you feed him for a day. If you teach a man to fish, you feed him for a lifetime. If you teach a man to teach others how to fish, you feed a whole tribe for lifetimes to come…"

Blessings and

L ots

O f

V aluable

E nergy

To you all…